The Learner-Centered Curriculum

The Learner-Centered Curriculum

Design and Implementation

Roxanne Cullen

Michael Harris

Reinhold R. Hill

Maryellen Weimer, Consulting Editor

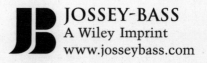

JOSSEY-BASS
A Wiley Imprint
www.josseybass.com

Published by Jossey-Bass
A Wiley Imprint
One Montgomery Street, Suite 1200, San Francisco, CA
94104-4594—www.josseybass.com

Jossey-Bass books and products are available through most bookstores. To contact
Jossey-Bass directly call our Customer Care Department within the U.S. at 800-956-7739,
outside the U.S. at 317-572-3986, or fax 317-572-4002.

Wiley also publishes its books in a variety of electronic formats and by print-on-demand.
Some material included with standard print versions of this book may not be included in
e-books or in print-on-demand. If the version of this book that you purchased references
media such as CD or DVD that was not included in your purchase, you may download this
material at http://booksupport.wiley.com. For more information about Wiley products, visit
www.wiley.com.

Library of Congress Cataloging-in-Publication Data
Cullen, Roxanne Mann.
  The learner-centered curriculum : design and implementation / Roxanne Cullen,
Michael Harris, Reinhold R. Hill Maryellen Weimer, Consulting Editor. — First edition.
    pages cm. — (The Jossey-Bass higher and adult education series)
  Includes bibliographical references and index.
  ISBN 978-1-118-04955-6 (cloth); ISBN 978-1-118-17100-4 (ebk.);
ISBN 978-1-118-17101-1 (ebk.); ISBN 978-1-118-17102-8 (ebk.)
  1. Education, Higher—Curricula—United States. 2. Curriculum planning—
United States. 3. Learning, Psychology of. I. Harris, Michael, date. II. Hill,
Reinhold R. III. Title.
  LB2361.5.C85 2012
  378.1'99—dc23
                                                        2011044979

Printed in the United States of America
FIRST EDITION
HB Printing   10 9 8 7 6 5 4 3 2 1

The Jossey-Bass Higher and
Adult Education Series

We dedicate this book to our families.

Roxanne Cullen dedicates this book to her husband, John.

Michael Harris dedicates this book to his wife, Tali, and his sons, Ronen, Asaf, and Amit.

Reinhold R. Hill dedicates this book to his spouse, Nell Rose, and to his three daughters, Zaida, Anja, and Kira.

Contents

Foreword

I am frequently asked in learner-centered teaching workshops whether one learner-centered course is enough to really make a difference in how students learn. The question is motivated by the fact that many courses at many institutions are still not learner-centered but continue to be teacher-centered and focused on content transmission. The questioner's sense is that even if a student has a different kind of learning experience in one course, that it won't be enough to make a significant difference and so maybe what's needed to make a course learner-centered is just wasted effort. Surprisingly, some research evidence is emerging that one learner-centered course early in the curriculum *can* make a difference (Derting & Ebert-May, 2010). Obviously, two courses will make more difference than one, a series would increase the impact still further, and a whole curriculum would be ideal.

The Learner-Centered Curriculum: Design and Implementation describes that ideal. It proposes how a learner-centered curriculum can be created, includes examples that illustrate what it might look like, and tackles the tough issues that surround curricular change. It's an inspiring book. Learner-centered curricula focus on the development of sophisticated learning skills. They don't just cover content but use what is known within a field to develop a strong knowledge base and to build the learning skills today's students will need for the lifetime of learning that awaits them personally and professionally. They are curricula that integrate knowledge across disciplines and topics. They combine the acquisition and application of knowledge with out-of-class experiences that give students opportunities to use what they are learning. They don't look like traditional curricula, and that's an issue.

Curricular change is never easy. For the most part, classroom are still teachers' castles. Behind their closed doors, they decide both what is taught and how it is taught. Sometimes well-intentioned academic leaders try to foist curricular revision on faculty. They require the submission and approval of course plans consistent with the new curricular goals and objectives. But then faculty return to their classrooms and pretty much teach the course as they've always taught it. Faculty have to want to change, and what makes this book more than just inspiring are the practical suggestions it offers for implementing these innovative curricula. The authors are (or have been) faculty members. They know how faculty members think about course design and curricular change. They offer approaches, arguments, and ideas that respond to faculty resistance to learner-centered approaches specifically and curricular change more generally.

This book can be profitably read by a variety of those in the higher education community. It can be read by that individual faculty member committed to learner-centered course goals who worries that one learner-centered course experience is not enough and wants there to be more. It can be read by curricular committee chairs and members. If a committee has been charged with curricular revision or even the possibility of it, this would be an excellent book for group discussion. It's a great book for department chairs. Learner-centered courses can be developed incrementally. Perhaps, given the politics of the institution or department, the best place to start is with two or three strategically positioned courses within a degree program. They can be taught by faculty committed to learner-centered goals, and this book discusses how those courses can be assessed and how that data can be used to motivate more curricular change. And certainly this is a book for academic leaders who aspire to change the curriculum at their institution. It makes compelling arguments as to why curricula need to be more learner-centered, and offers examples of those curricula and advice on setting the curricular change agenda.

The Learner-Centered Curriculum follows Leading the Learner-Centered Campus: An Administrator's Framework for Improving Student Learning Outcomes, written by Michael Harris and Roxanne Cullen. That book explores learner-centered leadership, proposing a leadership model based on the same learner-centered principles used with students and in classrooms. That kind of leadership sets the conditions for the curricular change described in this book. The two books are really companion works that move interests in learner-centered teaching from individual classrooms to institutions. It's common for institutions to claim they are learner- or learning-centered. These books make clear how that claim must be supported with policies, practices, and curricula that make learning the true centerpiece of an institution.

I also found The Learner-Centered Curriculum intriguing because it positions curricular change within a larger context. It isn't just about what is taught or even about how it's taught. It's also about where it's taught—what the classrooms look like, how technology should support learning goals, and how spaces around campus can be created so as to enhance the learning mission of the institution. Some of the richest examples are those derived from the authors' own experiences on their campus. They write about those with candor and insight.

Most of my work has been at the individual classroom level, and that's the focus of much of the literature on learner-centered teaching. Although that may be the easiest and most sensible place to begin, it is not the level at which significant change is accomplished. Learner-centered ideas have been widely promoted in the literature since Barr and Tagg's seminal article (1995). Unfortunately though, since then it has been mostly about trying to change higher education classroom by classroom. It's time to pick up the pace. Students deserve more than an occasional learner-centered experience. They should be able to participate in whole programs where how they are learning is just as important as what they learn. This book gives that conversation form and substance.

Maryellen Weimer

Preface

A few years ago, when the three of us were all working at the same institution, we took part in a classroom renovation project with the goal of making the classrooms more inviting and comfortable for students. With the aid of a design firm, we transformed sterile-looking, institutional white classrooms into colorful, technologically current learning spaces, with modern carpet design and state-of-the-art moveable furniture. Although this was a huge improvement over the rooms we had, we were limited by the existing spaces, and we could not reduce the number of seats in any classroom simply because of class sizes and increasing demand. The problem was that the most flexible furniture design in the world cannot be used to its true effect if confined in rooms that are too small. So, in many instances, our lovely folding tables with casters remain in their locked positions facing the front of the room.

We begin with this story because it serves as an analogy for the point we want to make about curriculum. Across the country, faculty are innovating and applying learner-centered practices in their classrooms. Too often, though, their courses are wedged into curricula that are not conducive to their innovations. Like a classroom that is too small for the specially designed furniture, the curricular model undermines the intent and restricts faculty members' ability to fully embrace learner-centered practices to the extent they might imagine. A second point is that the learning experience at an institution does not change if students take one or two learner-centered courses. If an institution is to be truly learner-centered, all processes and practices need to be learner-centered, and the curriculum is no exception.

In this book, we will consider ways to break down the walls that confine our imagination and, as in the case of physical spaces, redesign curricular spaces to support and enhance learner-centered teaching. We will make the case that for many existing programs, the curriculum design is predicated on elements of a paradigm that is contrary to what we are trying to achieve through learner-centered pedagogy.

Purpose

Many fine books on curriculum design already exist, and we reference many of them. We aspire to help faculty members and administrators think about curriculum in a new, learner-centered way. We have the same background as many of you. We are not instructional designers by training; we do, however, have extensive experience with curriculum revision from the faculty member's and administrator's perspectives. By exposing habitual ways of approaching curriculum, curriculum planners will become more intentional in their thinking and be able to develop a new approach that is more flexible and aligned with learner-centered pedagogy. Although we do offer suggestions and recommendations, our main agenda is to provoke thinking about how curriculum might be designed differently. In the end, our goal is to share our insights with those interested in joining us on our exploration of innovative, learner-centered curricula that prepare students, and the rest of us, for twenty-first-century teaching, learning, and careers.

Audience

It may be a quirk of English majors and avid readers, but those of us who pay attention to the books on people's bookshelves or to the books others are reading on a bus or park bench also make judgments about people based on those selections. If you are caught reading this book, we hope we know what people will think about you. At least we know what *we* think about you.

You are reading this book because you care about student learning. You may be frustrated that change in higher education takes so long, or you may be an agent of change trying to be innovative and creative in a system that often fails to accommodate your ideas. You see how rapidly the world is changing, and you want to make your students' educational experience relevant and current. You believe in learner-centered practices, and you want to apply them in new ways throughout your institution. You might be a faculty member interested in curriculum and desirous to make degree programs at your institution more learner-centered, or you might be a faculty developer whose job it is to provide others with curriculum design ideas. You might be a department chair or dean who would like to support curricular change in your unit, or you might be a provost or president who is trying to push forward the learner-centered agenda at the institutional level. Regardless of your role within the institution, you are open to new ideas and are looking for ways to improve the educational experience of your students, with the result being graduates who are prepared for the challenges we know they are going to face. We are writing this book to you and for you.

Structure

Because our aim is to foster intentional thinking about curricula, the first five chapters are organized around questions, specifically: *Why redesign curricula? How did we get to this point? What would a learner-centered design look like? How do we implement such a design? Where are they doing it already?* After explaining our thinking about these questions, we offer technical advice on how the strategic use of assessment, technology, and physical spaces can support a shift toward a learner-centered curriculum design.

In Chapter One, we reference the numerous calls for higher education to produce graduates who are creative, autonomous learners. We posit that creativity and learner autonomy can indeed be taught and that many of the practices we know as learner-centered pedagogy are consistent with the strategies used to develop creativity and autonomy.

In Chapter Two, we present a history of curriculum development and illustrate the ways in which this traditional design is based on an instructional paradigm derived from a mechanistic view of learning. We explore some underlying accepted assumptions about curriculum design, namely that curriculum is linear in design, that learning takes place the same way for all individuals, that time is an important factor in determining learning, that error is negative, and that knowledge is an entity to be owned and controlled.

In Chapter Three, we present a framework for curriculum design based on learner-centered principles. Using Doll's postmodern theory of curriculum as an organizing principle, we examine each of the assumptions presented in Chapter Two and offer learner-centered alternatives.

In Chapter Four, we explore implementation issues. We begin with a consideration of overarching principles related to curriculum implementation, and then we offer what we refer to as *What if?* conversations, intended to provide leaders with some specific questions to ask and consider in order to keep the conversation focused on new ways of conceiving curriculum and seeing the process from a learner-centered perspective.

Chapter Five provides examples of curricula that demonstrate the principles presented in Chapter Three. Using a rubric we developed as an instrument to gauge the degree of learner-centeredness in the design, we look at several curricula that illustrate varying degrees of learner-centeredness in their design and conclude the chapter with a hypothetical example of the revision of an existing program.

Throughout the book, we emphasize the need for assessment, noting specifically that both formative and summative assessments are key features of learner-centered pedagogy and that assessment is an effective driver of change. For that reason, we have devoted Chapter Six to assessment practices and offer a wide variety of options both for individual classroom practice and for programmatic assessment.

Chapter Seven is devoted to technology and the many new tools available to educators that can support learner-centered practices and foster autonomous learning. We make the point in Chapter Five that curriculum designs will necessarily vary in degree of learner-centeredness. In this chapter, we show how technology, particularly online learning environments, can assist in removing some of the obstacles to achieving a learner-centered design.

Learner-centered classroom pedagogy and curricula require physical spaces that are amenable to collaboration and engagement, so in Chapter Eight, we explore the importance of physical spaces in relation to learner-centered curricular design. We also recognize that tying renovation to curricular implementation can foster motivation to innovate, resulting in a physical manifestation of learner-centered principles.

Acknowledgments

We are grateful to the many individuals who have helped us during our research and writing. Our editor, Maryellen Weimer, brought profound assistance through her editorial expertise, her knowledge of the subject, and her conviction and enthusiasm for all things learner-centered. Working with her has been a joyful learning experience. We are also extremely grateful to David Brightman at Jossey-Bass for his support and facilitation of the project, and also to his assistant, Aneesa Davenport, and the production staff. Several colleagues spent considerable time reading drafts, listening to ideas, and offering suggestions. Their continued support has been a true blessing. Thank you Paul Blake, Lynn Chrenka, John Mann, Ric Underhile, and Leslie Wilson. Our book would be incomplete without the assistance of Stephen Durst, James Cohn, Wallace Murray, Eunice Chung, Gary Hauck, and Greg Wellman, who provided us helpful information on their programs and institutions. Thank you also to Nancy Larkin and Kathy Kennedy, who coordinated scheduling and provided untold administrative support. Finally, we acknowledge and express gratitude to the many students, faculty, staff, and administrators whom we learned so much from and who helped us create the vision. And of course we give our greatest thanks to our families, who have supported us with their love, enthusiasm, and, most of all, patience throughout the creation of this work.

About the Authors

Roxanne Cullen is a professor of English at Ferris State University (FSU) and coordinator of the bachelor of integrative studies degree program. In her tenure at FSU she has also served as Writing Center director, administrative head of the Department of Languages and Literature, interim associate dean of the College of Arts and Sciences, and assistant and associate vice president for academic affairs. In addition to her administrative service, Cullen is a recipient of the university's Distinguished Teaching Award. She received her PhD in English from Bowling Green State University and her BA in English from SUNY Geneseo. In 2010, she coauthored *Leading the Learner-Centered Campus* with Michael Harris.

Michael Harris serves as the chancellor of Indiana University, Kokomo, and as a professor of public and environmental affairs, education, and business. He received his PhD in public policy from Indiana University, his master's from Tel-Aviv University, and his undergraduate degree in economics and business administration from Bar-Ilan University. He is a graduate of two of the Harvard Graduate School of Education's leadership programs (IEM and MDP). He has published four books and close to forty articles in a variety of journals. Harris has been recognized for his teaching excellence, research, and service. He serves as a political commentator to a variety of broadcast and print media. Harris has been acknowledged nationally for his work in leading change and enhancing innovation and entrepreneurship. He has initiated a variety of projects that brought together international and local partners from government, business, higher education, and nonprofits to enhance academic excellence, student success, and economic development.

Reinhold R. Hill is dean of the College of Arts and Sciences at Governors State University in University Park, Illinois. Prior to his current position at Governors State, Hill held several administrative appointments at Ferris State University, where he began his full-time career in the Department of Languages and Literature. He earned his BA in communication studies with a minor in English at Brigham Young University. His MA is in English with a folklore emphasis from the University of Southwestern Louisiana. He earned his PhD in English with emphases in folklore and composition studies from the University of Missouri. Hill has regularly taught a full range of courses, including World Folk Literature, Introduction to American Folklore, Composition Theory, American Religious Traditions, Introduction to Literary Studies, and all levels of writing, including a proposal writing course, in both the traditional classroom and online. He was a Fulbright Senior Lecturer at the University of Debrecen in Hungary in 2004.

The Learner-Centered Curriculum

1

Why Redesign Curriculum?

Igor Pušenjak, age thirty-four, was placed fourteenth on *Fast Company*'s 2010 list of the one hundred most creative people. He and his brother designed Doodle Jump, the most popular application for the iPhone. The brothers' $100 investment, coupled with tenacity in the face of five previous failures, led to the game's selling more than four million copies by May 2010. On his Web site, Pušenjak describes himself as a "photographer, multimedia artist, designer, technologist, pilot, and an avid sailor," a modern renaissance man. Pušenjak's place on the *Fast Company* list points to the increasing importance of creativity and adaptability to changing work opportunities.

How does this story relate to curriculum design? Lattuca and Stark (2009) believe that looking at curricular change over time reveals that universities are reactive to societal pressures—that curriculum is a reflection, in fact, of its sociocultural context. We believe the time is right for major change in the design of curriculum because of the impact of current social reality and because of the research on learning that can inform the process. Furthermore, the success story of the Pušenjak brothers illustrates two recurring themes that directly impact curriculum design. First, the brothers were not trained in the area of their success; they integrated multiple talents and knowledge bases. Second, they were resilient in the face of failure and no doubt learned from their failures, which eventually led to their success with Doodle Jump.

In this chapter, we will offer our answer to the question, *Why do we need to redesign our curricula?* Beginning with an exploration of the current and future need for employees who are creative, independent learners, we will then consider how the traditional view of curriculum as a vehicle for transmitting knowledge is counterproductive with regard to the goal of developing graduates with those qualities. Next, we present documentation that supports the belief that creativity and adaptability can be taught. We answer the "Why redesign curricula?" question by demonstrating how realigning traditional curriculum with a learner-centered paradigm has the potential to create learning environments that are conducive to supporting independent learning and creativity.

The Call for Creativity and Adaptability

The societal need for autonomous learners who adapt quickly to new situations, who are engaged in lifelong learning, and who are flexible and innovative in their approach to problem solving is well documented (National Leadership Council for Liberal Education and America's Promise, 2007). A national survey conducted by Peter D. Hart Research Associates for the American Association of College and Universities asked employers to rate new hires in the skills that are generally agreed on to represent the abilities necessary to succeed in the twenty-first-century workforce. The results looked like a bell curve: not many A's or F's, mostly mediocre. Although these results may indicate that the United States is not in the dire circumstances that some have claimed previously, they do show that employers are not completely satisfied either. The results of this survey as well as the findings of other business and industry studies and independent educational research teams all indicate that higher education needs to do a better job of preparing students.

In its publication *College Learning for the New Global Century*, the National Leadership Council for Liberal Education and America's Promise (2007) outlines four broad areas in which all students should be prepared: (1) knowledge of human cultures and the physical and natural world; (2) intellectual and practical skills, including inquiry and analysis, critical and creative thinking, written and oral communication, quantitative literacy, information literacy, teamwork, and problem solving; (3) personal and social responsibility, including civic knowledge and engagement—local and global—intercultural knowledge and competence, ethical reasoning and action, and foundations and skills for lifelong learning; and (4) integrative learning, including synthesis and advanced accomplishment across general and specialized studies. Although the publication focuses on developing general education programs to address these areas, these general education outcomes can also serve as the structure of a reasonable degree program that develops in students an appreciation for and fluency with diversity in all its forms and prepares them for engagement in an increasingly globalized society. Of particular interest to us in regard to curriculum is the call for integrative learning.

As the report states, "In a world of daunting complexity, all students need practice in integrating and applying their learning to challenging questions in real-world problems," and continues, "In a period of relentless change, all students need the kind of education that leads them to ask not just 'how do we get this done?' but also 'what is most worth doing?'" (National Leadership Council for Liberal Education and America's Promise, 2007, p. 13). These perspectives are widely agreed on at the present time, but it is not always clear how we might arrive at the stated outcomes. The report authors argue,

> The general public—and many college students—continue to believe that choosing a "marketable" major is the key to future economic opportunity. Guided by this conviction, many students see study in their major field as the main point of college, and actively resist academic requirements that push them toward a broader

education. Many policy makers hold a similar view of career preparation, evidenced by their support for occupational colleges and programs that promise initial job readiness but not much else.

Those who endorse narrow learning are blind to the realities of the new global economy. Careers themselves have become volatile. Studies already show that Americans change jobs ten times in the two decades following college, with such changes even more frequent for younger workers. Moreover, employers are calling with new urgency for graduates who are broadly prepared and who also possess the analytical and practical skills that are essential both for innovation and for organizational effectiveness. (pp. 15–16)

As early as 1994, Bridges claimed that the concept of job security was a thing of the past, that today's workforce is operating by a new rule system, a new paradigm in which all workers are contingent and that a worker's value to an organization must be proven on a daily basis. Graduates can no longer expect to spend an entire career with one company climbing the corporate ladder, but rather must think of themselves as in business for themselves and maintain a career-long professional development plan. And this new workplace is a project-based team environment that demands agility and adaptability on the part of the worker. Bridges (1994) wrote, "These new rules are still evolving and are becoming operative in some parts of the economy more quickly than others. . . . At Sun Microsystems, Apple Computer, Intel and hundreds of smaller high-tech companies, these rules are already obvious" (p. 52). His predictions proved correct.

IBM conducted a global study of the elements needed for enhancing workforce performance in today's turbulent environment. From their survey of four hundred organizations in forty countries, the researchers concluded that the key to enhanced workforce performance was "an adaptable workforce that can rapidly respond to changes in the outside market" (IBM Global Services, 2008, p. 1). In other words, we need workers who are creative and who can adapt and solve problems in new ways. Yet creativity and adaptability have not been a major focus in the undergraduate experience.

Bronson and Merryman (2010) claimed in a *Newsweek* article that American creativity is actually declining. They make the point that while other countries are making creativity a national priority, we're headed in the opposite direction. The authors further note that student scores on creativity tests are dropping at the same time that their IQ test scores are rising. So the question remains, what needs to change in our education system in order to develop creative problem solvers for this world of daunting complexity? Bronson and Merryman pointed to the ironic state of educational reform. Currently the Chinese are replacing their "drill and kill" teaching with problem-based learning. At the same time, we are continuing to argue about standardized curricula, rote memorization, and nationalized testing. These authors noted that "overwhelmed by curriculum standards, American teachers warn there's no room in the day for a creativity class. Kids are fortunate if they get an art class once or twice a week" (p. 3). And herein lies the problem with our current way of thinking about creativity as well as about curriculum. First is the assumption that fostering creativity is the sole domain of a single discipline, namely art education, and second is the knee-jerk response to a curriculum issue: add a course.

Legislators and others continue to call for more tests in order to drive the needed changes in undergraduate education. More evaluation of the current curriculum will not foster needed change. To use an agricultural metaphor, calling for more testing is like trying to make the sheep fatter by weighing them more often when what they need is a richer pasture. Supplementing the current undergraduate diet with additional courses in global knowledge and critical thinking or creativity will not address the need either. What is needed is a redesigned undergraduate educational experience that will foster creativity as well as learner autonomy.

Can Creativity Be Taught?

Feldman, Czikszentmihalyi, and Gardner (1994) make the case that creativity has multiple meanings, which can sometimes impede communication, so we will begin by defining what we mean by creativity. They define their use of the word as "the achievement of something remarkable and new, something which transforms and changes a field of endeavor in a significant way. In other words, we are concerned with the kind of things that people do that change the world" (p. 1). The most accepted general definition is simply the "production of something original and useful" (Bronson & Merryman, 2010). We like Franken's definition of creativity as "the tendency to generate or recognize ideas, alternatives, or possibilities that may be useful in solving problems, communicating with others, and entertaining ourselves and others" (2006, p. 396), because it aligns most closely with our curricular goals and is probably a more reasonable way of thinking about teaching creativity. We are not expecting every student to change the world, but we can expect every student to recognize ideas and alternatives and learn to solve problems in new ways. Gardner (2006) described creative people as those who take risks without fear of failure while seeking the unknown or challenging the status quo. We will return throughout the book to the idea of taking risks with this attitude toward failure, in regard to creating suitable educational environments that foster creativity. Environment is key, as Czikszentmihalyi (1996) asserts. He maintains that creativity is tied to context—to interactions of talented people in an environment that is open and accepting of innovation. The role of environment will also serve as a theme throughout as we focus on environments that are conducive to learning.

In summarizing one hundred years of research on creativity, Plucker (2008) found that creativity more often than not involves teams and collaboration. Creative environments are collaborative and active. Feldman, Czikszentmihalyi, and Gardner's belief that reflection is the single quality that sets humans apart from other organisms (1994) is key to understanding creativity. In discussing the learner-centered curriculum, we will return to the concepts of risk taking, attitude toward failure, collaboration, and reflection as we consider ways to create curricula that respond to the need for creative thinkers.

Czikszentmihalyi's theory as to the role of context and cultural attitude toward creativity is reflected in a recent book that addressed creativity and innovation from a cultural perspective. Senor and Singer (2009) examined the Israeli phenomenon of entrepreneurism. Israel produces more start-up companies than China, India, Korea, Canada, and the United Kingdom in spite of what would appear to be limitations of size, geographical location, and perpetual political turmoil. The authors explain that Israel's impressive economic growth is a result of a unique mind-set. The Israeli mind-set, what some might call chutzpah, is an outgrowth of unique political and social realities. Senor and Singer attribute this mind-set for entrepreneurism to the military service that all citizens experience, coupled with the incredible diversity of cultural backgrounds within Israel. The military experience gives young Israelis a social range, a sense of responsibility, initiative, and agility of mind as well as ease with confronting authority, challenging accepted ways of doing things, critically analyzing and learning from mistakes, and assuming risk. Although the Israeli military experience may not be intentionally designed to foster creativity, there are certainly lessons to be learned. First, the experience creates an intense sense of community. Senor and Singer claim that the military experience creates a lifelong networking system that young Israelis capitalize on once their military experience is over. Control is also a key feature of the experience.

The young Israelis are expected to confront authority, they are given tremendous responsibility, and competence is expected. There is an acceptance of mistakes, provided that the individual learns from the mistakes and maximizes his or her potential as a result. In short, the environment fosters creative thinking.

Creative thinking thrives in environments that offer individual freedom, alternative thinking, safety in risk-taking, and collaboration and teamwork. Gardner (2008) noted in regard to educational environments and creativity that

> Too strict adherence to a disciplinary track operates against the more open stances of the synthesizer or the creator. Options need to be kept open—a straight trajectory is less effective than one entailing numerous bypaths, and even a few disappointing but instructive cul-de-sacs. (p. 84)

In other words, the educational path needs to be more flexible and integrative.

Creativity requires seeing possibilities, seeing from a new perspective, and perceiving difference, or what Langer (1989) would call mindfulness. She defined mindfulness as the ability to create new categories and to maintain an openness to new information and an awareness of more than one perspective. Without these abilities, individuals become entrapped in habitual ways of thinking, solving problems, and seeing, thus leading them to miss new signals and opportunities. The ideal in teaching creativity as well as learner autonomy lies in teaching mindfulness, or, as Langer would define it, becoming attuned to our cognitive processes, thinking about what we perceive and deliberately noticing difference and distinctions in our observations. We will refer to this as intentionality, becoming aware of one's own process of learning.

Langer (1997) talks about the conditional and context-dependent nature of the world, cautioning against teachers' fostering a belief in one right answer. She writes, "Teaching skills and facts in a conditional way sets the stage for doubt and an awareness of how different situations may call for subtle differences in what we bring to them" (p. 15). In Chapter Three, we will discuss her research to support this belief. Svinicki (2004) also discusses the limitations on student learning as a result of believing in one right answer. What she refers to as the "illusion of comprehension" is, in part, the result of students using flashcards or rereading as a means of studying. "They find comfort in looking at the same material over and over, mistaking their recognition of it in familiar context with an ability to recognize it out of context" (p. 117). She contends that this is why it is important for students to *use* information rather than simply identify it. When they are required to *do* something with the information, to take it from the familiar context and introduce it to another context, their illusion of comprehension is revealed; that, she claims, strengthens motivation to learn.

The seventh of seven principles of excellence espoused by the National Leadership Council for Liberal Education and America's Promise is "Assess students' ability to apply learning to complex problems." The principle emphasizes both the student's ability to apply learning in multiple contexts and the assessment of student abilities. We will return to the necessity of applying skills in unfamiliar contexts, or transfer, in subsequent chapters, as it is a fundamental principle for assessing deep learning, a concept we will look at in greater depth in Chapter Three.

Csikszentmihalyi (1999) examined the role society plays in innovation and creativity and determined that

> creativity is not simply a function of how many gifted individuals there are, but also of how accessible the various symbolic systems are and how responsive the social system is to novel ideas. Instead of focusing exclusively on individuals, it will make more sense to focus on communities that may or may not nurture genius. (p. 335)

In other words, our classrooms as well as our institutions need to nurture creativity. Csikszentmihalyi recognized that creativity is the result of three elements in interaction: the individual, the cultural domain, and the social field, or those who pass judgment on the quality of the creative work. This implies that teachers, those who are the judges of the quality of creative work, can foster learning environments that support and encourage creativity through increasing the openness and flexibility of those environments and accepting learning from multiple sources. Rosenthal, Baratz, and Hall (1974) found that teachers' expectations about students' performance clearly influence that performance. Further, when students see their own teacher as more intrinsically oriented toward work, they perceive themselves as more competent and more intrinsically motivated. Langer (1997) concludes that students' intrinsic motivation and hence creativity are likely enhanced both by teachers' attitudes toward autonomy and self-direction in work as well as by their own ability to model those same behaviors.

New research in neuroscience is shedding more light on how creativity works. Bronson and Merryman (2010) summarize the research. They explain that creativity has been popularly thought of as a left-brain activity, but research is showing that it is in fact an activity involving both right and left hemispheres. When a person tries to solve a problem, the first brain activity involves sifting through familiar solutions and obvious facts, a left-brain activity. If the answer cannot be found there, the neural networks from the right side look for memories that might be relevant. Information that would normally be ignored by the left brain becomes available, thus widening the possibilities for solving the problem.

> A wide range of distant information that is normally tuned out becomes available to the left hemisphere, which searches for unseen patterns, alternative meanings, and high-level abstractions. Having glimpsed such a connection, the left-brain must quickly lock

in on it before it escapes. The attention system must radically reverse gears, going from defocused attention to extremely focused attention. In a flash the brain pulls together these disparate shreds of thought and binds them into a new single idea that enters consciousness. (p. 4)

These two modes, referred to as divergent thinking and convergent thinking, are what characterize creative thinking, combining new information with old, even forgotten ideas. "Highly creative people are very good at marshaling their brains into bilateral mode, and the more creative they are, the more they dual-activate" (p. 4). They integrate diverse thoughts in order to solve problems.

Recent experiments have shown that this dual activation of the brain is teachable. The University of Georgia, the University of Oklahoma, and Taiwan's National Chengchi University have independently studied creativity training exercises aligned with this science, all finding that creativity training works (Bronson & Merryman, 2010). Collaboration, creative problem solving, and problem-based learning have all been shown to increase creativity in children. This recent research supports what earlier researchers have maintained about creative learning environments: they must be flexible, free, open to unusual or divergent answers, and collaborative.

To summarize what we know about creativity, we know that it is a whole-brain activity that involves making connections between sometimes remote ideas. We know that the ability to do this is fostered through environments that are open and supportive of creativity and divergent thinking, and that teachers can either stifle or promote creativity in their students, through their own behaviors and through the learning environments they create.

To summarize what we know about whether creativity can be taught, we know that the attitude as well as the behaviors of teachers are key to creating an environment that fosters creative problem solving. Maintaining an openness to new ideas, a willingness to allow students to make choices in how to engage, and presenting information in a conditional way rather than assuming only one right answer are all strategies that teachers can use to foster creativity. We also know that employing active learning strategies and encouraging teamwork and collaboration enhance creative output.

Can Adaptability Be Taught?

In addition to the societal call for creativity is the call for adaptability. Adaptability has to do with autonomy, with individuals who can learn on their own. In fact, many of the same recommendations regarding educational environments that foster creativity are also known to develop learner autonomy. These learner-centered strategies aim at developing independent learners who can think critically and solve problems—who can sort out the world of daunting complexity. As early as 1975, Knowles recognized that transmission of knowledge to passive recipients was no longer a viable means of education. Knowles (1975) identified the importance of self-directed learning in regard to adult learners and emphasized that when individuals take initiative for their own learning, they benefit not only by learning more but by retaining more.

More recently, Candy (1991) differentiated between self-directed learning as an educational goal and self-directed learning as an instructional method. As a goal, self-directed learning refers to self-management and personal autonomy. As a method of instruction, it refers to learners' assuming increased control in formal educational settings as well as planning and executing projects outside the formal setting. Here we refer to self-directed learning as a goal of education. Cognitive psychologists refer to this as self-regulation, a skill that can be developed through the incorporation of pedagogical strategies built into curricular design. Self-directed learning is essential to the development of inquiry skills that individuals need in order to adapt to rapid changes in their environment and to manage the great influx of information to be learned.

Self-regulation is defined by cognitive psychologist Albert Bandura as the ability of an individual to regulate his or her progress in achieving learning outcomes. Garavalia and Gredler (2002), Schapiro and Livingstone (2000), and Zimmerman (2002) have demonstrated that self-regulation can be intentionally crafted in courses to produce significant growth in essential learning behaviors. Self-regulation can be fostered through carefully constructing learning environments that prompt students to elevate their knowledge. McCombs (1989) and Zimmerman and Schunk (1994) identified skills that typify self-regulation; they fall into three categories: self-observation skills, self-judgment skills, and self-reaction skills. Nygren (2007) explained that "the knowledge expertise becomes stronger as the learner transfers and applies the skill in slightly different contexts. Eventually the learner will be able to use the skill in a completely new and unfamiliar context" (p. 165). In subsequent chapters, we will consider ways in which transfer of learning to different contexts can be integrated into the design of curricula.

Why Change Curricula?

If individual teachers can incorporate pedagogical strategies in their classroom in order to foster creativity and learner autonomy, why do we need to revise the entire curriculum? We believe that relying on individual classroom efforts to change the learning environment on a programmatic, college, or institutional scale is not strategic and does nothing to link and integrate those individual experiences. We believe that for graduates to develop the skills we have referred to in this chapter, curricular coherence, repeated experiences, and reflection on learning across courses are necessary. The design of the curriculum needs to integrate learning experiences for students in order to facilitate their growth as creative, independent learners.

The Association of American Colleges and Universities (AAC&U, 2004) and the Carnegie Foundation for the

Advancement of Teaching issued a statement in which they defined integrative learning as the learner's abilities to "integrate learning across courses, over time, and between campus and community life" (p. 1). This statement grew out of a project called Opportunities to Connect, in which ten campuses were selected to experiment with a variety of integrated learning strategies—linked courses, capstones, service learning, and learning portfolios—to create the "institutional scaffolding" for integrated learning. There has been widespread success with many of these strategies, and the successes individual campuses have achieved have been the result of extreme effort and dedication on the part of individuals committed to improving student learning outcomes. Part of the reason that these achievements have required such expenditure of energy and creativity on the part of the implementers is that our existing institutional scaffolding, also known as curriculum, is not conducive to flexibility and creativity.

The disconnect between traditional curriculum design and current student learning is the result of our approach to curriculum as a mechanistic process rather than an organic one. In the instructional view of learning that we will examine in greater depth in Chapter Two, learning is assumed to be the result of the professors' dispensing the right ingredients—course content. Once all the content has been dispensed, the student is complete. We know, though, that learning is an organic process dependent on numerous variables, including a student's prior learning, learning styles, motivation, and so on. Our curriculum design needs to reflect the organic nature of the process.

Rather than thinking of course content as pieces of a puzzle or ingredients in a recipe, we might use the metaphor of a gardener, who tends to the plant and provides nourishment, fertile ground, and other conditions conducive to growth, but who must stand aside and watch the plant grow on its own. Curriculum in this view is flexible and focuses on those elements that provide the learner nourishment and the conditions conducive to growth. The goal of this curriculum framework is to develop autonomous learners. Specifically, the design of curriculum must shift from the traditional discipline-based approach in which types of knowledge (as in hours of general education versus hours in the discipline major) are at the core of the curriculum to a constructivist or learner-centered approach that focuses on the development of the learner.

The 1970s hosted a considerable number of experiments in curriculum designed to foster independent learning and interdisciplinary thinking. Many proved ineffective. What we propose differs in large part because of the significant advances in research on learning that have taken place since that time, the research that serves as the basis for the learner-centered agenda. The learner-centered agenda proposes to shift responsibility for learning to the student, with the added benefit of stimulating student motivation for learning. It lays the foundation for creating learning environments that foster learner autonomy as well as creativity.

The Learner-Centered Environment

Bransford, Brown, and Cocking (2000) identify four features characteristic of learner-centered learning environments; they must be "student centered, knowledge centered, assessment centered and community centered" (p. 153). In thinking about curriculum, educators tend to focus on knowledge and skills that students must acquire but rarely discuss the role of learners' attitudes and beliefs or the environment. When we speak of environment, we mean the surrounding influences, the set of conditions that have an impact on learning. There are a multitude of such influences, including the attitude or mind-set for learning that the learner brings, the impact of the student's prior learning, the culture of learning that is fostered, the physical environment, and more. The current efforts to transform educational environments toward learner-centeredness are to a great extent an attempt to motivate students to be intentional learners and to change their attitude about learning—to develop a new mind-set.

Alfred Binet, inventor of the original IQ test, is quoted as saying, "[Some] assert that an individual's intelligence is a fixed quantity which cannot be increased. We must protest and react against this brutal pessimism" (Shenk, 2010, p. 29). Yet probably most people continue to believe that they inherit their intelligence from their parents and that's that. A body of research from both neuroscience and psychology suggests that intelligence is not only malleable but capable of growing in response to specific environmental stimuli. Shenk concludes that "intelligence is not an innate aptitude, hardwired at conception or in the womb, but a collection of developing skills driven by the interaction between genes and environment" (p. 29). He asserts that the question of nurture versus nature should be replaced with an acceptance of both nurture *and* nature. "The dynamic model of genes times environment $(G \times E)$ turns out to play a critical role in everything.... We cannot embrace or even understand the new world of talent and intelligence without first integrating this idea into our language and thinking" (p. 27).

Most difficult to recognize and perhaps the most powerful belief that affects learning is the student's belief in his or her ability, or self-efficacy. Students with high self-efficacy are more persistent in their learning in the face of difficulties. They interpret failure not as a personal failing but as a single poor performance that can be overcome with hard work. A student's sense of self-efficacy depends on his or her type of goal orientation: toward learning goals or toward performance goals (Dweck & Leggett, 1988). Students who are motivated by learning goals accept error and are highly motivated to understand and conquer new concepts or material. Those motivated by performance goals are interested in demonstrating competency. They are less willing to take risks because they want to avoid failure in their performance. Dweck (2000) has described these two types of learners in terms of two theories of intelligence: the entity and incremental theories.

The entity theory (later referred to as the fixed mind-set) posits that intelligence is static. Individuals are imbued with certain intelligence or ability that cannot be acted on by effort. In contrast, incremental theory (later referred to as the growth mind-set) posits that intelligence is malleable and can be affected by effort. Dweck's research has shown that individuals' belief in their intelligence or ability level affects their motivation to learn and subsequently their success at learning.

Those of us who have worked with developmental students have seen firsthand the effects of students' belief that they can't learn something simply because they have not been successful at it in the past or have been told that they aren't good at it. We have also witnessed (perhaps not as often as we would like) the tremendous excitement and sense of reward these same students experience when they do succeed, for they have been freed from a belief that has sometimes prevented them from even trying to learn. This experience is not restricted to developmental learners by any means, but the successes with those students are sometimes more readily apparent. The point we want to emphasize is that if we are to create motivated learners, we must first convince them that they can in fact learn, that their intelligence is not fixed but expandable.

Directly tied to one's attitude about intelligence is how one responds to failure. According to Dweck (2000), individuals who subscribe to a fixed mind-set see failure as an indication of less intelligence. Therefore, those who have a fixed mind-set are less likely to take risks or approach challenging problems. They stick with what they can perform well in order to demonstrate that they are intelligent. Those who subscribe to a growth mind-set, in contrast, see failure as a challenge to be conquered. To paraphrase an old adage, when the going gets tough, the growth mind-set gets going! Gardner (2008) described this as a singular quality of creative individuals. He noted that the creator is perpetually dissatisfied with his or her current work, enjoys striking out in unusual directions, and is robust about failure.

> All of us fail, and—because they are bold and ambitious—creators fail the most frequently and often, the most dramatically. Only a person who is willing to pick herself up and 'try and try again' is likely to forge creative achievements. (p. 83)

Senor and Singer (2009) provided numerous examples of this approach to failure in their examination of the innovative mind-set of the Israeli military. They describe the debriefing process as a time to show what the individual learned from his or her mistakes. "The effect of the debriefing system is that pilots learn that mistakes are acceptable, provided they are used as opportunities to improve individual and group performance" (p. 94). Shenk (2010) claims that "in the sometimes counterintuitive world of success and achievement, weaknesses are opportunities; failures are wide-open doors" (p. 115). Failure provides an individual with an opportunity to examine his or her thinking and make adjustments. Therefore, in creating learning environments that are conducive to creativity, we need to be very attentive to our attitudes and reactions with regard to failure.

The teacher's mind-set is equally as important as the students'. In a study by Deci, Nezlec, and Sheinomy (1981), teachers' beliefs in the importance of student autonomy correlated significantly and positively with their students' preference for challenge, curiosity, and desire for independent mastery.

Creativity and the Power of Choice

Sharing power with students is a key factor in learner-centered practices as well as in developing creativity. Giving students opportunities to choose fosters engagement with content and helps ensure that they find activities relevant. The same is true in regard to creativity. Amabile's extensive study of creativity (1996) outlined the factors that affect creativity in learning environments. Most important is openness, both physically in terms of classroom configuration and metaphorically in terms of a sense of freedom and safety. We will address the impact of physical spaces for learning in Chapter Eight and offer examples of contemporary design that are open and flexible. Less structure and fewer teacher-initiated constraints also correlate with creative productivity.

It is clear that people support what they help build. Sharing power also increases student motivation, and motivation and persistence are key to innovation. Amabile (1996) addresses the relationship of motivation and creativity to power and control. She identifies three components related to people's creative output: (1) people's knowledge, experience, and talent in a given area; (2) their cognitive style—their energy, persistence, and ability to see new perspectives; and (3) their motivation. She reviews numerous studies showing that the factors that encourage intrinsic motivation are the same as those that motivate creativity.

She notes the difference between intrinsic and extrinsic motivation: "intrinsic motivation is conducive to creativity, but extrinsic motivation is detrimental" (p. 15). Extrinsic motivation arises when goals are imposed on the learner by others, when the learner feels powerless. Pink (2011) notes that this phenomena has been studied by psychologists, sociologists, and economists, all coming up with the same counterintuitive result. Rewards do not incentivize learning except in cases of performance of rudimentary mechanical skills. Once cognitive skills enter the problem-solving equation, then additional external rewards lead to poorer performance.

Rewards alone do not necessarily lead to enhanced performance. Although the type of reward may be a determiner, individual choice and control play an integral role as well. Amabile writes, "Choice can be an important mediator of the effects of reward on creativity" (p. 168). When individuals are given choice—not necessarily in *whether* to engage in an activity but choice in *how* to engage in an activity—creativity is increased.

An interesting illustration of this phenomenon takes place in the Australian software company Atlassian. One day per quarter, software developers are given total autonomy. They are told to create something however and with whomever they wish. The atmosphere is very open and fun, almost like a party. The only caveat is that they must present the results of their effort in twenty-four hours. What the company has found is that those twenty-four-hour sessions have produced an amazing array of creative ideas and new software solutions (Pink, 2011). The freedom to make choices regarding what to work on and whom to work with leads to tremendous creative output.

Choice is also part of learner-centered pedagogy. Learner-centered practices motivate learners by offering them control over their learning and creating a sense that the learning tasks have relevance. Learner-centered pedagogy fosters the sharing of power between students and teachers. When teachers offer students choices and responsibility and contextualize learning to increase the sense of relevance, the result is intrinsic motivation for learning and learning environments that are conducive to creativity and innovation.

Cognitive psychologists have added greatly to our understanding of motivation. Rather than seeing individuals as purely behavior-based organisms responding to positive and negative stimuli, psychologists have studied how motivation may be a function of interpretation. A cognitive view of motivation supports learner-centered pedagogy because it places motivation in the realm of the learner rather than treating the learner as the recipient of stimuli he or she then reacts to. Social cognitive theory places motivation in the mind and the environment of the learner.

Svinicki (2004) proposed an amalgamated theory of motivation that combines three prominent theories: the expectancy value model of Wigfield and Eccles (2000), the social cognitive model of Bandura (1997), and the goal orientation model of Dweck and

Leggett (1988). Svinicki explains that motivation is a balancing of the value of the goal and the expectation that the goal can be achieved. Both are motivators. "When students have the opportunity to make decisions for themselves, they are most vested in the outcomes of those decisions and therefore more likely to invest the effort necessary to make the outcomes happen" (p. 155). Furthermore, self-determination fosters self-confidence and self-esteem. She adds, "the degree that you can share control with them [students] you will have a more compliant audience" (p. 156).

Pink (2011) summarized research on motivation, noting that three factors lead both to better performance and to personal satisfaction: autonomy, mastery, and purpose. Autonomy leads individuals to become engaged in an activity as opposed to merely complying with someone else's direction. Mastery of tasks causes individuals to experience self-satisfaction. Pink uses the example of individuals who play a musical instrument for fun. They practice the instrument for hours and hours on their own time in order to improve. They do so because of the reward of improvement, not because someone is making them practice. The same is true for people who enjoy a sport or other activity that requires practice for mastery. There is intrinsic reward associated with making progress. Finally, people feel motivated to contribute to some greater good, to have a purpose to their work. As we noted earlier, in learner-centered pedagogy, this need for purpose is tied to making learning relevant to the student. When students understand the relevance of subject matter, they are more motivated to learn it.

Chapter Summary

We opened this chapter asking, *Why redesign curriculum?* Our answer: the shift toward learner-centered pedagogy represents an important step in the quest to develop creative, autonomous learners who can readily adapt to a rapidly changing society. Learner-centered techniques foster creativity and innovative thinking, absolutely essential abilities for today's workforce.

The institutional shift toward learner-centeredness is not a new idea. Many institutions make the claim that they are learner-centered; however, more often than not, that claim refers to pedagogy or individual efforts like those described in the AAC&U Opportunities to Connect project. In *Leading the Learner-Centered Campus* (Harris & Cullen, 2010), we made the case that the entire institution must shift its focus toward learner-centeredness if there is to be a true paradigm shift. All practices and processes in all divisions of the institution need to be part of that shift. If we confine the shift toward learner-centeredness to the individual classroom, we will limit its impact. To return to the analogy mentioned in the Preface, it would be like putting contemporary furniture conducive to collaboration in a tiered classroom. We need to consider the larger framework of the educational experience—the curriculum—and make efforts to design that curriculum such that the pedagogy of the individual classes maximizes its potential. The Wingspread Group on Higher Education made the following statement in regard to essential educational reform: "Putting learning at the heart of the academic enterprise will mean overhauling the conceptual, procedural, curricular, and other architecture of postsecondary education on most campuses" (1993, p. 14). In the remaining chapters, we will provide a framework for reconceptualizing curriculum in order to put learning at the heart of the enterprise, and in the final chapter we will address quite literally the architecture of postsecondary education.

2

Curriculum Design in the Instructional Paradigm

In this chapter, we examine curriculum design in relation to the instructional paradigm, the paradigm of modernism. Modernism emphasized the rational, the objective, the impersonal, and the fragmentation of thought and action. Hunkins and Hammill (1995) offer this definition: "It is a society of prizing and accepting certainty, a society privileging a mechanical view of the world. It is a society that employs the rational, the scientific in addressing problems of human life and society" (p. 17). This scientific and mechanistic frame of reference presupposes stability of knowledge and uniformity of process. When this frame is applied to education, we get the instructional paradigm, a view of learning that is characterized by control over individuals, ownership of knowledge, and a view of students as receivers of knowledge.

Since Barr and Tagg (1995) coined the terms *instructional paradigm* and *learner-centered paradigm* in their seminal article in *Change* magazine, there has been much talk of shifting paradigms, so much so that the magnitude of what is actually involved in shifting paradigms has been minimized to a great extent. Learning to see and understand the underlying assumptions of one's paradigm is no easy task. In *The Learning Paradigm College*, Tagg (2003) wrote of the tenacity of paradigms, likening them to a lens that modifies our vision. Removing that lens and learning to see in a new way are challenging because everything about the instructional paradigm is the norm, the way we have learned to perceive our reality. Brookfield (1995) concurred:

> Paradigmatic assumptions are the hardest of all assumptions to uncover. They are the structuring assumptions we use to order the world into fundamental categories. Usually we don't even recognize them as assumptions, even after they've been pointed out to us. Instead we insist that they're objectively valid renderings of reality, the facts as we know them to be true. (p. 2)

So part of our task is to challenge assumptions—in this case, the assumptions we make in designing curricula. We will begin by briefly examining the history of curriculum theory and design: What aspects have we come to assume to be facts or unchangeable realities? How has the instructional paradigm influenced our current practices? We will also examine changes in accrediting standards that will help support a new view of curriculum.

Curriculum History

Franklin Bobbitt is credited with presenting the earliest definitive work on general curriculum, *The Curriculum* (1918) and *How to Make a Curriculum* (1924). He applied the principles of scientific management—developed by Frederick Winslow Taylor for improving industrial efficiency—to curriculum development in order to create educational efficiency. His approach was to identify learning activities as the basis for curriculum decisions. He defined human life as consisting of the performance of activities, so education should prepare children for life; therefore, the "abilities, attitudes, habits, appreciations, and forms of knowledge that men need" became the objectives of a curriculum (Beauchamp, 1975, p. 65). Hunkins and Hammill (1995) assert that "perhaps his [Bobbitt's] greatest contribution is his argument that the process of curriculum-making is not specific to any particular content, but rather cuts across subject matter" (p. 17). We would add that Bobbitt's focus on activities and on tying outcomes and objectives to learning experiences is consistent with current thinking on learning.

It is Bobbitt's atomistic view of learning, however, that launches the factory view of education that characterizes the instructional paradigm. Schiro (2008) notes,

> In an analogy comparing curriculum development to the industrial manufacture of steel rails, Franklin Bobbitt [1918] laid bare the essentials of the social efficiency ideology. The school is compared to a factory. The child is the raw material. The adult is the finished product. The teacher is an operative or factory worker. (p. 59)

According to Schiro, Bobbitt's scientific method of curriculum development asserted that "curriculum should be developed in a 'scientific' manner similar to the way industry produces its products" (p. 61). He viewed the purpose of education as near-Orwellian in nature, as the training of individuals for specific functions. Although he included general education for life skills and preparation for citizenship, the majority of the curriculum comprised a number of vocational tracks to which students were assigned on the basis of testing.

Bobbitt believed that assessments of intellectual abilities were essential in discovering the individual's designated competency. His belief in predetermined skills and competencies represents the fixed view of intelligence that we discussed in Chapter One. Bobbitt later came to change his views on this, indicating that "neither he nor any other educator could predict the lives of students" (Hunt, Lasley, & Raisch, 2010, p. 838). He also came to believe in a more general education focused on the individual student's intellectual development rather than strict adherence to vocational preparation.

We made the point in Chapter One that society has a significant impact on curriculum development, and we emphasized that the shift toward a learner-centered paradigm is essential to meet the demands of a changing society. Bobbitt's view was a reflection of his time, in that he saw the primary purpose of education as a means of control. Doll and Gough (2002) note direct connections between the scientific management theories of Taylor and the curricular ideas of Franklin Bobbitt, Ellwood Cubberley, W. W. Charters, B. F. Skinner, Ralph Tyler, and Madeline Hunter. "In the writings of all these curricularists, control is preeminent: it is always preset, prior, and external to the learning activity itself" (p. 35). Doll and Gough go on to quote from Taylor's fourth law on the relation between management and labor. Management gives orders, and labor follows the orders, in regard not only to what is to be done but how it is to be done and when it should be done. Doll and Gough claim that the underlying purpose of education in this view is to control individuals, to "change behavior patterns of people to acceptable norms" (p. 36).

Tyler's *Basic Principles of Curriculum and Instruction* (1949) epitomizes the technical aspects of curriculum that characterize modernism. Tyler's scientific technique is a direct outgrowth of Bobbitt's early work. What became known as the Tyler Rationale is a linear, cause-effect model of curriculum building that still predominates today. "Tyler gave us a techno-speak that enabled us to be part of the modernism of this century" (Hunkins & Hammill, 1995, p. 18). This modern perspective on curriculum reflected attitudes of the time. Doll (1993) commented that it was predicated on a positivist certainty, a rational and stable view of reality that resulted in curriculum development as a mechanical procedure. We need to make an important qualification here in regard to Tyler. Tyler identified three criteria for effective design: continuity, sequence, and integration. As Wiggins and McTighe (2005) point out, "Tyler explicitly warns that the typical sequential approach of marching through content chronologically in history does not pass the test of intelligent continuity" (p. 298). In short, the Tyler Rationale, when reconceived from a postmodern point of view, lays the groundwork for curriculum designed around learners' experiences, a design we will examine further in Chapter Three.

A persistent argument in curriculum design has been one of *content* versus *process*. Beauchamp (1975) notes that "the original dichotomization of the terms content and process probably occurred over arguments about whether teachers should be predominantly concerned with a body of content to be learned by pupils or with pupil learning processes" (p. 112). There has been widespread acknowledgment by educational researchers that curriculum content should be organized according to established disciplines. "This is the culture content, or organized knowledge, generated by those who have worked in the discipline" (Beauchamp, p. 114). Those who pushed for "discipline-centeredness" believe that the discipline scholars are the ones who should be responsible for curriculum planning.

Schiro (2008) explores how four competing visions of education have given rise to competing views of curriculum. These four visions arise from disparate beliefs regarding the type of knowledge that should be taught, the nature of learners, how teachers should teach, and how learners should be assessed. He labels these four ideologies as follows: the *scholar academic* ideology, the *social efficiency* ideology, the *learner-centered* ideology, and the *social reconstruction* ideology. In higher education, the scholar academic ideology has persisted, rising out of a view that a single epistemological position exists about knowledge; that is,

> knowledge exists "out there" external and independent
> of the knower. It is as if knowledge is a jigsaw puzzle
> that can be shaped into multiple parts; even though
> different representations can be drawn, the pieces of the
> puzzle are the same to all of the organizational players.
> For students to become engaged they must learn the
> different pieces of the puzzle. (Tierney, 1995, p. 36)

In this view, curriculum is owned by the faculty and dictated by discipline specialization. Content knowledge sits at the center of curriculum design, and those responsible for curriculum review examine the knowledge of the discipline as well as the amount of time devoted to individual units of knowledge. Curriculum design in this paradigm is focused on the transfer of discipline knowledge to students and on the time devoted to that transfer.

Disciplines and Divided Communities

Academic disciplines are more than collections of content knowledge. Disciplines are communities, communities governed by their own paradigms, and in the instructional paradigm, the differences between them more often lead to competition and rivalry than to cooperation and support. Disciplines are hierarchical in organization, another characteristic of the instructional paradigm. Scholars rule from the top of the hierarchy, where they fulfill their role as researchers discovering new knowledge. Below them reside the teachers, whose role is to disseminate that knowledge, and at the bottom reside the students, who are in the process of learning the discipline's knowledge so that they may become a member of the discipline (Schiro, 2008). Schiro refers to a "territorial imperative" at work in disciplines, whereby students are potential property, and members of the discipline are not inclined to share the domain of their schooling with rivals. Moran (2005) stated this more bluntly: "Disciplines, therefore, are about power, hierarchy and control in the organization of knowledge" (p. 74).

The experience of a colleague in the humanities illustrates this discipline-based territoriality. He proposed a literature course in folklore for general education designation and sought two designations, cultural enrichment and social awareness. He was denied the social awareness designation, despite the fact that the content of the course was clearly focused on the relationship of the literature to different societies and that folklore is often considered a social science discipline. The course designation was denied because it would not be taught by someone in the social science discipline as defined by that department. The decision held in spite of the fact that our folklorist colleague had graduated from a folklore program housed in social sciences.

Henry (2005) explored the concept of disciplinary hegemony, noting that although "integrative and interdisciplinary studies programs, departments, or colleges embody the essence of best practices that enhance student learning and prepare students for the complexity of real world issues, they are also highly vulnerable to institutionalized disciplinary hegemony" (p. 4). Integrative and interdisciplinary programs are especially vulnerable because of the power historically vested in academic disciplines. Rogers, Booth, and Eveline (2003) argued that because academic disciplines have overseen control of content and pedagogy, they have in fact controlled the organization of higher education, defining higher education as we know it today.

Fuchsman (2007) asks, "How do we get [away] from disciplinary fragmentation and specialization; from the 'kingdom of knowledge' as Rustom Roy says, being 'balkanized, nay feudalized, divided into a hundred fiefdoms'?" (p. 2). The major undertaking of learning a discipline requires acculturation to the language, modes of thinking, historical tradition, and mode of inquiry associated with that body of knowledge. It is by its very nature a process of differentiation. However, because of political realities, budgetary concerns, or sometimes fundamental philosophical differences, people within differing discipline communities are often at odds with one another. (After one very fractious meeting between two departmental curriculum committees, a colleague who is a chemist wrote a highly amusing treatise on why biology was not a science.)

The ever-increasing specialization within disciplines also exacerbates turf wars. We witnessed a decade-long battle over who would teach educational psychology, the School of Education or the Department of Psychology, with the end result being that both taught it but to different audiences. If an education student made the mistake of taking the psychology course, the student would be required to retake the course from the School of Education. Course duplication is a common phenomenon arising from the divisiveness of the instructional paradigm. Another colleague told us that there are four competing courses in Web design on her campus—four courses in three different colleges, all covering the same basic material. We expect that these examples sound familiar and perhaps have triggered memories from your own experiences.

The Instructional Paradigm and Curriculum

As we observed in our historical overview, the instructional paradigm is predicated on an industrial model of human learning, literally a factory model of education. This view of learning prizes quality control, which is ironic, considering that higher education is currently under such intense scrutiny to be accountable for the quality of graduates. A recent criticism issued in a report by the American Association of University Professors (2008) placed the factory analogy in a contemporary perspective, noting that as U.S. colleges and universities are "embracing the operating strategies of for-profit corporations with growing fervor ... [they] increasingly conceptualize higher education as a commodity and attempt to provide it at the lowest cost. They do so by reorganizing themselves as 'knowledge factories'" (p. 12).

In this paradigm, quantifiable measures such as ACT, SAT, and HSGPA determine student potential, deeming the student to be the acceptable raw material for our product. Quality control is especially evident in the freshman year, during which the weaker material is sorted out. The Wingspread Group on Higher Education (1993) charged that "our education system is better organized to discourage students—to weed them out—than it is to cultivate and support our most important national resource, our people" (p. 5). This established practice of determining student potential is an outgrowth of the entity theory of intelligence and reminiscent of Bobbitt's early views on learning.

In Chapter One, we introduced Dweck's distinction between entity and incremental theories of intelligence (2000). The entity theory posits that intelligence is static. Individuals are imbued with certain intelligence or ability that cannot be altered by effort. The instructional paradigm fosters this view of intelligence, resulting in educational environments that are not conducive to risk-taking and innovation. Individuals who believe that intelligence is static focus on proving that they are as intelligent as their IQ test indicates they should be, rather than challenging that assumption and performing above their assigned level of intelligence. These individuals tend to be less aggressive problem solvers, seeing mistakes as flaws in intelligence rather than as opportunities for growth. Teaching becomes a matter of disseminating information and then grading students' ability to retain it.

Curriculum in this model is an inflexible, fixed collection of courses occurring in a prescribed, linear sequence, with little opportunity for electives or deviation. And characteristic of the business or factory model, if a student does require a substitution of courses, he or she must submit a form with multiple signatures of approval. This mass production mentality requires students to assimilate information at equivalent rates with equivalent responses, thus devaluing individual differences. The assembly line conception of education presupposes students' sameness, diminishing the importance of prior learning, individual differences, and extracurricular experiences. Each student follows a common path or progression of courses with the goal of emerging from the assembly line.

In relying on a modernist conception of knowledge and reality, the instructional paradigm views knowledge as a quantifiable commodity that can be isolated, identified, transmitted, and controlled. We see this in the traditional division of units, departments, and colleges according to academic discipline, the knowledge that is owned by the discipline. Tagg (2003) writes that departments have replaced faculty as the core of educational institutions and that faculty members' influence on student learning is exercised through academic departments: "At most colleges, academic departments hire faculty members, and academic departments in the Instructional Paradigm college derive their power from their role as depositories for classes" (p. 23).

We all have stories of academic turf wars. There is probably no issue more divisive on college campuses than general education. The American Association of Colleges and Universities (AAC&U) devoted an entire session of one of its annual conferences on general education to "strategies and politics for general education reform." Gaff (2004), who has written widely on the subject, identified some of the key factors that make general education such a knotty issue. He describes general education as "that ill-defined portion of the undergraduate curriculum that belongs to nearly everyone and is the sole province of no one" (p. 1). Gaff points to budget as a key issue in the general education turf wars:

> The faculty committee that oversees the general education curriculum, if the institution has one, tends to draw those interested in internal institutional service and those committed to preserving the resources accruing to their departments from the general education program. . . . More often, such faculty governance arrangements become the venue for determining which courses are approved to "count" as meeting general education degree requirements, thereby ensuring the offering departments and their faculty fully-enrolled, full-time-equivalent revenue-generating courses. Such subsidies have little to do with the aims, purposes and assessment of student learning in general education. (p. 2)

A colleague described to us the discussion at her academic department meeting over ongoing general education reform. The gist of the discussion was that the department felt threatened by general education reform because students might not have to take the currently required math course if programs across campus made the case that their discipline-based statistics courses counted as quantitative knowledge. No one was able to turn the discussion around to student learning. The fear of losing new positions as a result of reduced productivity dominated their thinking. Concern over territory and ownership prevailed.

In an even more dramatic example, the university-wide discussions of general education reform became so heated and embittered on one campus that the provost imposed a two-year moratorium on revision of the general education curriculum and even on further discussion of the issue.

In sum, the factory model of education has fostered a mechanized rather than organic approach to student learning; it is an approach that conceptualizes knowledge as a commodity. The logical extension of this view is that knowledge, the commodity, can be owned.

Ownership of Knowledge

The belief that knowledge can be owned exerts its influence on various processes within the university, among them hiring, promotion and merit, and, of interest here, curriculum development. The core belief of shared governance suggests that faculty, because of their academic expertise and generally long-term commitment to an institution, should regulate academic standards of curriculum. Shared governance maintains academic integrity by preventing political or commercial interests from influencing institutional decision making, with the discipline-specific professional organizations serving as the primary safeguards against outside pressure. The adherence to academic standards established by the discipline, rather than by the individual institution, balances and integrates standards across institutions. Although we recognize the importance of shared governance, its manifestation within the instructional paradigm has contributed to a mind-set that has fostered unnecessary divisiveness and fragmentation.

The effect of this belief that knowledge is both owned and distributable is evident in the curriculum review process, in which, in some instances, professors are asked to delineate how many minutes per semester will be devoted to individual topics within the course outline, or accrediting bodies ask for the number of hours per semester devoted to specific knowledge. Tagg (2003) referred to this as educational atomism:

> In the "educational atomism" of the Instructional Paradigm, the parts of the teaching and learning process are seen as discrete entities. The parts exist prior to and independent of any whole; the whole is no more than the sum of the parts, or even less. The college interacts with students only in discrete, isolated environments, cut off from one another because the parts—the classes—are prior to the whole. A "college education" is the sum of the student's experience of a series of discrete, largely unrelated, three-credit classes. (p. 110)

If we look at curriculum manuals, documents meant to guide faculty in developing or revising new courses or programs, we typically find a complicated process with numerous gatekeepers. Course developers are often required to provide reviewers with a considerable amount of data, including such information as the presence of similar offerings at neighboring institutions or similar programs on their own campus. They are often asked to speculate on the effect the new program might have on enrollment, the number of expected majors, and the need for additional faculty and additional facilities, as well as on the budget implications of these effects. Budget and territory emerge as the primary focus. Although these are necessary considerations in program development, they tend to dominate the process. Student learning is at best assumed and at worst not considered at all. As we explore the possibility of a new, learner-centered paradigm, we begin to see how anachronistic the instructional paradigm is and the ways it limits and constricts us.

Five Underlying Assumptions

What then are the assumptions that we have accepted as a result of working under the influence of the instructional paradigm? **Assumption one** posits that curriculum needs to be linear because learning is a linear, additive process. However, research on learning, some of which we reviewed in Chapter One, indicates that learning isn't quite the neat and tidy process we may have assumed it was.

Bruner (1960) described the ideal curriculum as a spiral that asks learners to revisit concepts repeatedly. This concept grew out of a constructivist philosophy of learning. Constructivism arose from Piaget's dynamic constructivist theory of knowing and has taken various forms, such as radical constructivism (von Glaserfeld), social constructivism (Gergen), social cultural constructivism (Bruner), and social constructivism (Vygotsky). In general, constructivists believe that learners construct knowledge rather than receive it, and the act of construction is greatly dependent on the prior knowledge and experience that the learner brings to the task. Von Glaserfeld (1995) explains, "from the constructivist perspective, learning is not a stimulus-response phenomenon. It requires self-regulation and the building of conceptual structures through reflection and abstraction" (p. 14).

The constructivist philosophy has been supported by research from various disciplines. Biological researchers Leamnson (1999), Sylwester (1995), Zull (2002), and Willingham (2009) have aided in defining the brain's functions in relation to learning, demonstrating the role of prior learning. Distinctions between memory and knowledge and depth of knowing have been explored by various researchers (Marton & Säljö, 1976; Marton, Hounsell, & Entwistle, 1977; Entwistle & Entwistle, 1991; Ramsden, 1988, 1992; Langer, 1997; and Bowden & Marton, 1998). And as we mentioned in Chapter One, a number of psychologists and educational researchers (Bandura, 1986, 1993, 1994, 1997; Biggs, 1987, 2003; Bruner, 1960; Gardner, 1983; Csikszentmihalyi, 1996,

1999; Covington, 1992; Conway, Perfect, Anderson, Gardiner, & Cohen, 1997; Driscoll, 1978; Dweck & Licht, 1980; Svinicki, 2004; Dweck & Leggett, 1988; Dweck, 2006) have contributed greatly to our understanding of learners and the role of memory, self-regulation, self-efficacy, and motivation in learning. Collaboration among learners is believed to be more productive than independent learning because learners construct knowledge using the varying backgrounds of the community members (Bruffee, 1995). Key here is the importance of relevance to learning and of establishing a sense of a community of learners.

The evolution of composition studies provides one example of how educators challenged the assumption that learning, in this case learning to write, was a linear, logical process. The traditional way of teaching writing was a logical, rational, linear approach that involved teaching grammar rules to students. The students were expected to follow those rules, and if they did, they would presumably write well. Students were given a procedure to follow: (1) develop a thesis and an outline to guide your writing, (2) write the paper, (3) read it over and apply the rules you've been taught. As researchers began studying the composing processes of students as well as those of professional writers, however, they found that few writers actually compose according to this linear description; instead, many writers follow a recursive process that is not easy to describe and may deviate depending on the rhetorical situation. For many, writing is an act of discovery through which the writer comes to understand his or her thesis or thinking on a topic. Through the assessment and study of actual writing processes, researchers came to understand and promote the importance of revision, collaboration, reflection, and rewriting. Although the transition wasn't easy, composition pedagogy did change to reflect the reality of how writers write and took into consideration the individual differences among writers.

Assumption two underlying the instructional paradigm is that everyone learns in the same way and that if we deposit the information into students (to borrow from Freire's banking analogy), then students will know the information and know it in the way we presented it. Learner-centered views on learning are derived from research in psychology that point to two major trends regarding how learning occurs. The cognitive constructivist view revolves around the individual's construction of knowledge or mental structures. Sociocultural constructivists focus more on the social and cultural interactions that affect the individual's construction of knowledge. Both views see knowledge as actively constructed by the individual through a process of self-regulation and recursive examination of his or her knowledge through interpretation and testing. Learning involves self-organization by the learner through a process of reflection and dialogue—thus the need for a spiral or other nonlinear design for curriculum.

Assumption three credits time with a role in learning, and the time it takes to learn is somehow indicative of one's intelligence. Tagg (2003) addresses the role of time in the instructional paradigm, observing that time is the constant and learning is the variable. Our system of education is obsessed with time. We parcel out the minutes in a course over weeks in a semester that are then equated to credit hours. We have prescribed the numbers of hours in degrees. Accrediting bodies look at the amount of time devoted to specific subjects within degree programs. A colleague used to refer to credit hours as the coin of the realm. In the instructional paradigm, credit and time are equivalents.

Assumption four is that error is negative. In a factory model of learning, mistakes are to be avoided because they are indicators of flawed thinking. To return to Dweck's entity and incremental theories of intelligence, we know that those who ascribe to an incremental theory of intelligence believe that intelligence is expandable, that it can grow. According to this view, error is positive; it is an opportunity to learn and to expand one's intelligence. Shaughnessey (1977) defined this shift in thinking in her now classic work, *Errors and Expectations*. She showed how errors in student writing are simply indicators that the student is operating under a different rule system; it is the role of the teacher to discover that rule system and to teach the student in reference to his or her existing rule system. Errors open the door to understanding a person's thinking process and are thus central to helping students learn. Constructivists refer to this as the disequilibrium that fosters learning. Error is not to be avoided but rather embraced as an indication of the learner's construction of knowledge.

Assumption five states that knowledge is an entity to be owned, controlled, and disseminated according to discipline-specific rules. We tend to organize curricula according to discipline and discipline history. If a student moves from one discipline to another, he or she more often than not loses credit hours because the hours—the coin of the realm—do not transfer into the new discipline. There is no credit-hour equivalent to the euro. The knowledge of one discipline is not valued in another.

To summarize, we have identified five assumptions about learning that have traditionally guided people's thinking about curriculum: (1) that learning is a linear process, (2) that knowledge can be transmitted to learners, (3) that how long it takes someone to learn something is indicative of his or her intelligence, (4) that error is negative, and (5) that knowledge is an entity to be controlled and owned. There has been, however, considerable research arising from multiple disciplines to refute each of these assumptions. In this section, we have introduced you to some of this research, but we are still left with a challenging question: *How do we promote curricular change?*

And herein lies the most difficult issue to confront: change. Psychological research has shown that even in the face of evidence, individuals will hold on to their current belief system unless there is a compelling advantage to accepting a new one. In subsequent chapters, we will offer a compelling advantage to adopting a new conception of curriculum, one that we believe is more conducive to student success and holds the promise of creating a more cohesive environment for faculty and administration. There is a second motivator for accepting this change, and this one comes from accrediting bodies. In the remainder of this chapter, we will describe the impact that new accrediting standards are having in driving curricular change.

Accrediting Bodies and Curricular Change

Accrediting bodies have the capacity to drive curriculum, and much to our good fortune, many accrediting bodies are beginning to recognize the shortcomings of older standards of review and have taken actions to alter their approaches. The Accrediting Board for Engineering and Technology (ABET), for example, has taken important steps in addressing the need for change, increasing the focus on student learning outcomes. Prados (1991) described the development of new standards as a response to the growing realization that the existing criteria were too prescriptive and rigid, and inhibited innovation.

ABET's new standards, known as EC2000, require programs to set clear educational objectives, collaborate with industry, conduct outcomes assessment, and feed data from these assessments back into the program for continuous improvement. The goal of this revision was to effect program change in the areas of curriculum and instruction, faculty culture, and policies and practices impacting student experiences in and out of the classroom, thus having an impact on outcomes both in student learning and employer ratings of new hires. ABET predicted that a shift in accreditation criteria would drive curricular reform, and research indicates that incremental change has taken place. At the request of ABET, Penn State's Center for the Study of Higher Education studied the impact of the reform. The report (Volkwein, Lattuca, Terenzini, Strauss, & Sukhbaatar, 2004) of the center's three-year assessment provided promising data on the effect accrediting criteria have had on curriculum change.

Although faculty and program chairs agreed that engineering program curricula changed considerably following implementation of the EC2000 criteria, the overall focus was entrenched in the traditional paradigm fixated on adding content rather than on embedding and redesigning curriculum. Few programs experienced any reduction in current emphasis, especially in the foundational topics in mathematics, basic science, and engineering science, yet indirect measures suggested an increased emphasis on nearly all of the professional skills.

Accrediting bodies overseeing health-care-related programming have made similar changes. According to the National League for Nursing (2006),

> Student-centered, interactive, and innovative programs and curricula should be designed to promote leadership in students, develop students' thinking skills, reflect new models of learning and practice, effectively integrate technology, promote a lifelong career commitment in students, include intra- and interdisciplinary learning experiences, and prepare students for the roles they will assume.

The Accreditation Council for Pharmacy Education (ACPE) imposed changes in 2007 that have motivated pharmacy programs across the country to revise their curricula, two of which we will look at closely in Chapter Five. These changes were inspired by the collaborative work of the standing committees of the American Association of Colleges of Pharmacy (AACP), which is documented in "Roadmap to 2015: Preparing Competent Pharmacists and Pharmacy Faculty for the Future" (AACP, 2006). Leaders in the profession acknowledged that the emphasis of pharmacy education must move beyond the narrow aspect of knowing the right drug for the right patient to a patient-centered and population-based model of care. The ACPE changes emphasized three main areas:

1. The standards sought to refine processes in order to ensure the development of students who can work collaboratively with

other health care providers to contribute to the care of patients. This accreditation goal reflects the learner-centered emphasis on active learning and collaborative learning and on understanding multiple contexts.

2. The revised accreditation standards also place greater emphasis on a scientific foundation coupled with practice competencies organized around outcomes assessment to enhance the development of students as lifelong learners. This goal coincides with the learner-centered focus on experiential learning and assessment of learning outcomes.

3. The standards endorse a holistic view of students' professional knowledge, skills, attitudes, and values; they also endorse sound and reasoned judgment and the highest level of ethical behavior. This goal is consonant with the learner-centered emphasis on learner autonomy and on deep learning that enables learners to transfer knowledge from one context to another.

Both the nursing and pharmacy accrediting bodies call for more experiential learning, more attention to critical thinking and problem solving, and educational settings that are learner-centered, interactive, and innovative.

The Higher Learning Commission (HLC) of the North Central Association, formerly the Commission on Institutions of Higher Education, has undergone numerous changes and revisions since its inception in 1895. In 1913, it first began accrediting colleges and universities with the goal of assuring quality. Its focus was on standards that were predominantly prescriptive and quantitative. Recognizing that this approach limited experimentation and creativity, the commission changed its focus, shifting from uniform standards applied to all, to a criteria-based model that allows institutions to be judged against their own goals and purposes. Rather than an *inspection*, the accreditation became an examination of norms derived from collected data. Over time, accreditation has continued to become more qualitative than quantitative.

Now, for example, institutions have a choice between two avenues for review, the Program to Evaluate and Advance Quality

(PEAQ) and the Academic Quality Improvement Process (AQIP). Both avenues require institutions to provide evidence, both direct and indirect measures of student learning. Criterion 3 of the PEAQ review addresses student learning and effective teaching. Organizations are asked to provide evidence that they have goals for student learning in the form of outcomes and that these goals and outcomes are clearly stated for each program. Institutions are asked to provide evidence that they support effective teaching, create effective learning environments, and offer learning resources to support both student learning and effective teaching.

Although changes made by accrediting bodies certainly represent a positive move on their part, building a culture of assessment takes time. Some institutions still do not understand the difference between direct and indirect measures, and they continue to accumulate data but never close the loop and use the data to drive change. We will address in Chapters Four and Six some of these issues in relation to building a culture of assessment. The changes that have been made by these bodies open the door for experimentation and creativity in curricular review. Both PEAQ's and AQIP's criterion-based form of review allows for the flexibility to redesign curricula according to learner-centered, constructivist principles.

Chapter Summary

In this chapter, we have examined the underlying influences of the instructional paradigm on traditional curriculum design, among them the following assumptions: (1) that knowledge can be owned and distributed, (2) that all individuals learn in the same way, as receivers of knowledge, (3) that the time it takes someone to learn something is important, (4) that error is negative, revealing one's lack of intelligence, and (5) that knowledge is owned and disseminated according to the rules of individual academic discipline. In the remaining chapters, we will challenge these assumptions and offer specific mechanisms for doing so. Curriculum reviewers and designers can benefit from the advances made by accrediting agencies, for many of these agencies have already moved away from this narrow and restricting view of education.

3

The Learner-Centered Curriculum

In Chapter Two, we examined curriculum through the lens of the instructional paradigm in order to challenge some of our assumptions about curriculum design. We identified several widely held and troublesome assumptions: that curriculum design needs to be linear; that knowledge is transferable; that time is an organizing principle; that error is to be avoided; and that knowledge is owned and controlled by discipline. O'Banion (1997) refers to the architecture of education that we have inherited as one that is time-bound, place-bound, efficiency-bound, and role-bound, and states that

> there is almost universal agreement that these bonds must be broken if the schools are to be redesigned and reengineered to place learning first.... There are many other factors, of course, that must change if the schools are to be transformed, but the transformation of the structural elements is essential. (p. 9)

There is perhaps no more central structural element than curriculum, and if we are to transform our institutions to be truly learner-centered, then we must address curriculum design.

In this chapter, we will use Doll's postmodern theory of curriculum (1993) as an organizing principle for a curriculum design based on recent research on learning and creativity and learner-centered practices. We will challenge each of the assumptions we identified in the previous chapter and describe the characteristics of curricula designed according to learner-centered principles. Such curricula will focus on the individual's process of learning to become an autonomous learner, which results in a graduate who is adaptable, innovative, and creative.

New times call for new curricula, and, as we discussed in Chapter One, those times are upon us. The modern era presupposed a stability to the universe. Hunkins and Hammill (1995) wrote about the worldview of modernism, saying that "life could be viewed as mechanical, that there existed a stable-state universe, that goals could be separated from the experiences designed to address those goals" (p. 20). Postmodernism, in contrast, sees the universe as organic and dynamic, not stable. Hunkins and Hammill put it this way: "We are in a time that is encouraging the projection of new meanings and suggesting ways to organize these myriad interpretations. The times, being identified as postmodern, are encouraging the achievement and employment of multiple awarenesses" (p. 20).

Take, for example, the shift in the presentation of historical events from modern to postmodern times. We have shifted from an acceptance of one "story" to the recognition that events have multiple interpretations depending on the point of view of the participants. The American revolution, for example, is told from two very different points of view depending on whether one is looking at a standard U.S. school textbook as opposed to a typical Canadian textbook. Or consider the modern versus postmodern views of Christopher Columbus.

Curriculum design seen from this postmodern, constructivist view is a significant departure from the traditional conception of curriculum as dispensing a single reality or perspective of knowledge to learners. The postmodern view instead focuses on the learners' construction of knowledge and the transfer of that knowledge within different contexts. In Chapter One, we used the metaphor of the teacher as gardener, calling for a more organic view of learning. We will seek a more organic view of curriculum design as well. The postmodern focus emphasizes the use of knowledge as opposed to the acceptance of it. Various theorists have proposed models for postmodern curricula. As we noted, we will use Doll's model (1995) as a way of organizing the research on learning that informs a learner-centered curriculum. He presented four criteria for postmodern curriculum design: richness, recursion, relations, and rigor.

Postmodernism and Curriculum Design: Richness

By richness, Doll (1995) meant that the experience of education should be enriching, examining layers of meanings and interpretation of experience. He said, "The paramount feature of the postmodern curriculum is openness.... It needs to be rich enough in depth and breadth to encourage meaning making" (p. 63). In his view, designing curriculum is a creative process, and the key to making the curriculum rich is dialogue among participants. Doll also talked about the need for depth in curriculum, quoting Whitehead: "Do not teach too many subjects, but what you teach, teach thoroughly. Let the main ideas which are introduced be few and important and let them be thrown into every combination possible" (p. 65).

The concept of deep learning grew out of the research of Marton and Säljö (1976) and described a way of learning that integrated new information into existing knowledge, leading learners to adopt new perspectives and understanding. In Chapter One, we discussed the need for students to be able to transfer knowledge from context to context, and in this chapter we have acknowledged the postmodern worldview that recognizes multiple contexts. When students learn something at a deep level, they have integrated it into their existing knowledge and have enriched or even revised their understanding. Because this knowledge is fixed in relation to other existing knowledge, they can draw on it and apply it in multiple contexts.

Svinicki (2004) clearly explains the difference between shallow and deep processing. Shallow processing relies on surface features. When we try to remember students' names, we often rely on physical features or some other association that aids us in retrieving that information readily. Unless we develop a fuller knowledge of that student as a person, we will more than likely forget the student's name after the semester is over. This type of shallow processing is what students do when they cram for an examination. They manage to store the information in their working memory long enough to get through the test, but they have not integrated it into their network of understanding, their long-term memory, the consequence of which is what a colleague referred to as the rapid forgetting that characterizes the typical undergraduate education.

Deep processing, in contrast, requires long-term storage. When deeply processing information, students are making connections between what they are learning and what they already know or, more precisely, making connections between working memory and long-term memory. The more someone already knows about the subject, the easier it is for him or her to deeply process new information about it. Willingham (2009) explains that this is the reason why using analogies is such a productive way to foster understanding, for through the analogy, the learner is able to relate the new information to something familiar. He further explains why concrete examples help convey the meaning of abstract principles: "We understand new things in the context of things we know, and most of that is concrete" (p. 67). This is why learner-centered practice suggests that teachers assess students' prior learning and try to relate new knowledge to the students' current understanding. Svinicki (2004) notes that "this is one reason why it is so much easier to teach upper division courses or adults: The learners bring a lot of prior knowledge with which to connect, so the instructor doesn't have to make connections for them" (p. 28).

This is not to say that prior knowledge can't also be an impediment, particularly if the prior knowledge is incorrect or inconsistent with the current information. A simple illustration of this is students' typical understanding of comma usage. Typically, if you ask students when to use commas, their reply is, "when I pause while reading." This method of inserting commas presupposes that students are proficient readers and that they will miraculously pause at the appropriate syntactic moment. Helping them understand that commas are about the eyes of the reader, not the ears of the writer, can be a challenge. Although they may accept the idea that commas function as a visual aid enabling readers to recognize the subject and syntactic structure of the sentence more easily, students are usually more comfortable with their established way of doing things. The new way of thinking about commas requires understanding grammatical structures, introductory phrases, and independent clauses, all of which is new territory for many students and requires work and learning. The old way of playing it by ear is far easier, so convincing them to leave that way behind is often unsuccessful; and, after all, in the minds of most students, a comma error is not a major issue.

Deep processing is in a sense breaking a habit, a way of doing something or thinking about something that we have used, practiced, become accustomed to. Svinicki (2004) cites Posner, Strike, Hewson, and Gertzog's research (1982) on the conditions necessary for individuals to accept a conceptual change: the previous belief must no longer be satisfactory, and the new belief must be intelligible, plausible, and fruitful—that is, it needs to work as well as or better than the old. This is, of course, what we are asking you as readers to do: to accept a conceptual change in the way you view curriculum, to leave behind a prior understanding.

Biggs (1987) and Ramsden (2003) noted that the conditions for learning established by the instructor can affect the learner's ability to adopt these strategies for deep learning. As educators, we can create conditions that facilitate deep learning, thus creating a transformative experience for students. Deep learning requires an investment on the part of the learner, who employs a synthesis of learning strategies, including discussion with peers, reflective writing, practical application, and reading in order to fully process information, with the added benefit of retaining and transferring information at higher rates (Biggs, 1987, 2003; Entwistle, 1981; Entwistle & Ramsden, 1983; Prosser & Miller, 1989; Ramsden, 2003; Tagg, 2003). Tagg described deep learning as follows: "Deep learning is learning that takes root in our apparatus of understanding, in the embedded meanings that define us and that we use to define the world" (p. 70). Active learning strategies that require sense making, self-assessment, and reflection are key to fostering deep learning (Bransford, Brown, & Cocking, 2000).

Although we can see how this might be accomplished in the individual classroom, we need to ask ourselves, *How can curriculum design foster deep learning?* Bransford, Brown, and Cocking (2000) identify three important elements for designing learner-centered environments: what is taught (the content), why it is taught, and what mastery or competence looks like. Wiggins and McTighe (2005) apply these elements to curriculum design and compare focusing on content to focusing on the understanding of content—that is, deep learning. They simply ask designers to become more thoughtful and specific about purpose. "Our lessons, units and courses would be logically inferred from the results sought, not derived from the methods, books and activities with which we are most comfortable. Curriculum should lay out the most effective ways of achieving specific results" (p. 14). Designers should work backward from the competencies to see that learning has taken place. They first identify desired results, then determine acceptable evidence, and finally plan learning experiences and instruction. In Chapter Five, we will show how active learning strategies, self-assessment, and reflection are built into curriculum design.

Postmodernism and Curriculum Design: Recursion

Doll's second feature of postmodern curriculum is recursion (1995). Recursion suggests a nonlinear approach to curriculum, whereby students reflect on their learning over time, examining how their understandings change and become altered with the accumulation of knowledge and experience. Too often in the linear curricular model, students have an attitude of getting things out of the way. General education requirements, for example, are for some a hoop to jump through before they get to the interesting material within the major. We laugh with our colleagues when students complete their English requirement and assert, "I'm done with English," as if they will never again use their native language. The conception of a nonlinear curriculum has been described as a matrix, a spiral, and a sphere, the point being that there is no clear beginning and end; the learner continues to revisit and reconsider his or her learning.

The spiral curriculum is not a new idea. Wiggins and McTighe (2005) note that its roots go back to Kant, Rousseau, and Hegel as well as Piaget and Dewey, though it is most commonly associated with Bruner (1960), who asserted that learning is an active, social, and reciprocal activity. Knowledge is not an unchanging body of information that is transmitted to learners. Instead, learners actively engage with knowledge over periods of time, revising, reflecting, and actively constructing their understanding in the context of their accumulated knowledge and experience. For Bruner, the learner transforms experience into learning. This learning is not done in isolation but as part of communal activity and sharing of perspectives and cultures.

We assume that if you are reading this book, you are interested in student learning. Your own evolution as a teacher or administrator has no doubt changed over time. Ours certainly has. As we continue to learn more about our discipline and about student learning and behavior, and as we engage in dialogue with our colleagues, our teaching practices and approaches typically change—we hope for the better. Teachers of literature, for example, often read classic works many times over the span of a career, and their understanding and interpretation of the text often changes over time as they interact with the text at different points in their life and in different social realities.

Wiggins and McTighe (2005) describe the spiral design as follows: "A spiral approach develops curriculum around recurring, ever-deepening inquiries into big ideas and important tasks, helping students come to understand in a way that is both effective and developmentally wise" (p. 297). They further note that although this design has rarely been implemented, the time may now be right as a result of need and of advances in learning theory.

In Chapter One, we touched on the concept of learner motivation, citing Svinicki's amalgamated theory of motivation. Motivation to learn and to be an autonomous learner is tied to one's goals and one's anticipation of success. It is also tied to one's active engagement in the process of learning. Svinicki (2004) recommends that at the course level, learners become actively engaged in the process of understanding information rather than relying on the instructor to carefully construct learning tasks and content organization.

> In this model it is best to have the learners create their own examples, structures, and understandings. The learners are much more actively involved than the instructor in going through the steps of learning.... [F]rom a cognitive perspective, those answers will be more meaningful because they draw on the learners' own experiences and world views. They are more likely to be deep processed answers, because it is the learners who have put forth the effort to identify key ideas and make key connections. (p. 36)

This is not to say that students are simply left to their own devices. Wiggins and McTighe (2005) emphasize the need for teachers to help students see the hierarchy of content and recognize that all content is not equally important. A learner-centered curriculum will ask students to become actively engaged in the design of their learning experiences, to create their own goals, to create linkages between courses and other learning experiences, and, as we will show in Chapter Five, even to design their own curriculum.

In designing a learner-centered curriculum, designers must sort out what Wiggins and McTighe (2005) refer to as the "big ideas" and structure the curriculum around these big ideas, which may mean relinquishing some content that has been considered necessary in the old curriculum. This brings us back to Whitehead's suggestion to teach fewer ideas deeply rather than cover lots of content quickly. Wiggins and McTighe recommend that programs and courses be organized around "essential questions, enduring understandings, key performance tasks and rubrics," all of which become the blueprint for design (p. 275).

Postmodernism and Curriculum Design: Relations

In referring to relations, Doll (1995) sees the relationship between parts as more important than disconnected units. Curriculum creation becomes a social activity involving considerable reflection and discussion. It is creative and full of *play* in terms of flexibility and elasticity. According to Doll, the linear curriculum is a continuum of particles, whereas the postmodern curriculum replaces particles with relations, "a gathering or matrix of interrelated 'occasions'" (p. 65). As we noted in the previous chapter, the discipline-centered curriculum discounts knowledge from outside the discipline; therefore, students who change majors lose credits. In the postmodern curriculum, there is no unnecessary knowledge that gets discarded if a student changes majors: all knowledge is necessary and personalizes one's understanding.

The learner-centered curriculum takes into account the postmodern view of the universe and thus recognizes the complex, idiosyncratic, and personal nature of learning. The process of learning involves the individual's seeing things from multiple perspectives and understanding the effect of different contexts. Likewise, Usher and Edwards (1997) note, "Education in the post-modern era, based as it is on cultural contexts, ... cannot help but construct itself in a form which would better enable greater partici-pation in a diversity of ways by culturally diverse learners" (p. 212).

A former student described an experience he had at a local community college. He identified the experience as pivotal in his understanding of and appreciation for the general education requirements. In order to "get it out of the way," to use his words, he registered for a political science course at the community college close to his home during the summer term. As a nontraditional student from the College of Technology, he resented having to take a social awareness distribution requirement, but with no recourse, he signed up for a course that fit his work schedule; in other words, he had absolutely no interest in it. In the class, there were three young women who were Bosnian refugees. One assignment required students to give oral presentations on a world leader whom they admired. Each of the three Bosnian women chose Bill Clinton.

Our student was taken aback. His predominant thinking about Clinton had to do with the president's personal indiscretions while in office. As the women recounted the terrible suffering they en-dured and the sense of being saved, literally, by the Clinton policy to intervene, our student began reconsidering his beliefs. He said that he had never really separated the personal from the professional and had not been able to see that Clinton had achieved some important accomplishments in spite of what the student believed was behavior on Clinton's part that embarrassed the country. This experience most likely would not have taken place had the professor simply presented the Clinton policy on Bosnia. The presence of the Bosnian women telling their stories from their perspective challenged the student's belief on a personal level because he had to try to reconcile his personal contempt with their adoration, both views having considerable weight.

Contexts can also be thought of in terms of frames of reference, or meaning structures. According to Mezirow (1991), a frame of reference has two dimensions. First is habits of mind, which are "broad-based assumptions that act as a filter for our experiences" (p. 17). These are usually assumptions or opinions that we have accepted without critically examining them, often cultural or social attitudes—our paradigm. An example of this is the role that home ownership plays in the American dream. Without really thinking of the options, opportunities, and limitations that accompany home ownership, people accept the social norm that home ownership is preferable to renting. Florida (2010) makes the point that the only reason that home ownership is so deeply ingrained as the attainment of the American dream is that public policy has placed it there for the benefit of several industries.

The second dimension of a frame of reference is the resulting point of view: "these include our points of view, attitudes, beliefs and judgments as they intersect with our sense of self" (Mezirow, 1991, p. 18). Returning to the home ownership example, individuals gain a great sense of self-satisfaction and attainment, a perceived sense of freedom when owning their own home. Home ownership becomes intertwined with one's sense of self and success, regardless of how constraining and financially draining home ownership might actually be.

As learners become aware of their own frames of reference and then become aware of the frames of reference that others employ, they gain perspective and deepen their understanding. This is what Langer (1989) referred to as recognizing multiple perspectives: "The consequences of trying out different perspectives are important. First we gain more choice in how to respond.... Second, when we apply this open-minded attitude to our own behavior, change becomes more possible" (p. 71).

She illustrated this with a psychological experiment that she conducted in which individuals were presented with simple objects—a rubber bone, for one. One group was told, "This is a dog's chew toy." The other group was told, "This could be a dog's chew toy." Each group was then asked individually to fill out some forms in pencil. The researcher pretended that some mistake had been made and that they would have to reschedule the session when they had new forms to use. Each individual who was told, "This could be a dog's chew toy" solved the problem by using the rubber bone as an eraser. No one in the other group thought to do that. They had been limited by the suggestion of a single perspective. This type of study has been replicated in various forms. Langer's point is that when individuals are presented with a single reality—"This is a dog's chew toy"—they are limited by the context; when individuals are presented with more open interpretations, however, they problem-solve and respond more creatively. The simple suggestion of doubt—this might be a chew toy, but it might not be—leaves open the opportunity to see in new ways. Recognizing multiple perspectives is essential, and as Langer's work indicates, the presentation of material can have a significant impact on learners' ability to perceive multiple contexts.

Postmodernism and Curriculum Design: Rigor

Rigor is what creates richness, according to Doll (1995). The postmodern use of rigor is less about being strict or severe and more about being persistent and thorough in examining one's understanding. Doll asks curriculum creators to be intentional in their design and to continually question their assumptions and actions. In regard to Doll's conception, Hunkins and Hammill state,

> It appears that the model of curriculum development
> implied by Doll has the features of being self-organizing
> as opposed to mechanistic, of being non-linear in action
> compared to linear, of being conducive to creativeness
> and openness as opposed to being deterministic, and
> drawing its essence from chaos theory as opposed to
> Newtonian mechanics. (p. 24)

Jencks (1992) argues that this model of curriculum acknowledges complexity and creativity. Rigor in curriculum design refers to elements that provide learners opportunities for integrative learning—that is, learning that is organized around problems or issues rather than strictly discipline content. By integrative learning strategies, we mean inquiry skills, critical thinking, problem solving, and experiential learning, all of which develop learner autonomy and persistence. When learners become autonomous, self-directed, and persistent in their learning, they develop strategies for lifelong learning. These skills enable them to function in our rapidly changing society, for as we noted in Chapter One, the twenty-first-century workplace calls for flexibility and adaptability as well as lifelong learning. Workers need to learn independently and to transfer knowledge from one context to another—in other words, to have processed information deeply enough to apply it in new contexts.

White (1982) proposed a view of curriculum designed to develop learner autonomy. He argued that the purpose of education is to assist individuals in living a whole life and having the capacity to be fulfilled. The major problem associated with this concept of the individual's ability to make good choices that lead to that individual's leading a full life resides in the definition of what constitutes a full life. Our use of the word *autonomy* is related not to one's ability to lead a full life but rather to one's ability to learn independently. How one chooses to employ those powers is beyond the scope of our discussion.

A curriculum with rigor is integrative. The concept of integrative learning is not new. It grows out of the progressive movement that advocated a problem-centered curriculum. Dewey (1956) also advocated for a curriculum that blended a focus on the learner with the needs of society as well as content specialty. In *Curriculum Integration: Designing the Core of Democratic Education*, Beane (1997) provides a history of curriculum integration, pointing out numerous advantages, including increased student involvement because of their role in selecting content, increased student achievement because of the focus on learning and making connections between course content and their personal lives, and better preparation for life because of collaborative experiences and broader understanding of principles and concepts.

Bernstein (1971, 1990, 1996, 2000) also explored the concept of an integrated curriculum, one in which the boundaries between content areas were not rigid. Bernstein believed that the relationships between categories or disciplines is more important than the contents within those categories. He also made a distinction between horizontal knowledge, one's everyday knowledge, and vertical knowledge transmitted through schools and academic disciplines. An interplay between the two is essential if students are to construct knowledge and perceive relevance as they build on their current knowledge base. Most essential is the degree of control students have over the choice, organization, and access of content (Bernstein, 1971).

Beane (1995) also makes an important distinction when considering integrated curriculum and the academic disciplines. According to him, the question of whether the academic disciplines are at odds with integrated curriculum design is at the heart of the issue, and he believes that rather than seeing the disciplines as opposed to integration, we should see them as a "useful and necessary ally" (p. 616). He defines curriculum integration as the search for what knowledge is for:

> Curriculum integration begins with the idea that the sources of curriculum ought to be problems, issues, and concerns posed by life itself. I have argued elsewhere that such concerns fall into two spheres: 1) self- or personal concerns and 2) issues and problems posed by the larger world. Taking this one step further, we might say that the central focus of curriculum integration is the search for self and social meaning. (p. 616)

He further argues that the problem is not with the academic disciplines themselves but with the presentation of them as separate from one another. The academic disciplines offer, in Beane's words, "a lens through which to view the world" (p. 617), along with a community that shares a way of seeing and interpreting the world. The disciplines, therefore, provide contexts for the learner, and designing a curriculum that favors the integration of these contexts over the separateness of disciplines is fundamental to creative thinking. An integrated curriculum should allow for the sharing of perspectives among disciplines and across time.

This approach to discipline integration may seem naïve or idealized in light of the discussion of disciplinary hegemony in the previous chapter, but as we noted in that discussion, the integration of disciplines represents best practices in teaching and learning, practices that transcend disciplinary boundaries. A colleague described her experience in defending her minor in film studies by using research on learning. During the academic program review process, our colleague, the program coordinator for the film studies minor, was questioned regarding the elective options offered to students. The issue involved the number of courses other than film that students could elect, raising the question of whether or not the minor was truly film if a student could essentially take more courses in television production, literature, popular culture, and communication than film courses. Rather than delving into the question of discipline and what constituted the discipline of film studies, she instead focused her response on the need for multiple perspectives in understanding film as an art form. She cited research similar to what we cited in Chapter One and in this chapter, emphasizing the depth of learning that results from examining the multiple influences on film production. The result was a thoughtful discussion of student learning and an enlightened program review panel.

The political reality of territoriality among the traditional disciplines and newly integrated programs, particularly in times of economic stress when disciplines find themselves fighting for diminishing resources, cannot be ignored. Not all disputes are resolved as easily as our example of the film minor; however, framing such a discussion in terms of the documented evidence of recent research on learning creates a forum for discussion that offers the possibility of diminishing that territoriality and shifting the focus of discussion away from disciplinary content and toward student learning. We will look more closely in Chapter Four at the impact of the politic when we examine implementation issues.

We have chosen Doll's four characteristics—richness, relations, recursion, and rigor—as an organizing principle for learner-centered curriculum design because they provide us with a framework for addressing the five challenges to traditional thinking about curriculum that we identified in the previous chapter. Furthermore, Doll's characteristics integrate well with the research on learning that underpins the learner-centered agenda. As we mentioned previously, we cannot expect anyone to leave behind the instructional paradigm unless we offer a place to go that is profitable. We believe that there is much to be gained from curriculum design focused on learner-centered principles, the most important gain being better-prepared graduates.

Postmodernism and Curriculum Design: Seeking Integration

Integrative learning is both a postmodern curriculum feature, what Doll called rigor, and one goal of learner-centered pedagogy, so we present integrative learning here as a bridge between the postmodern theory of curriculum and the research on learning that defines the learner-centered agenda. Integrative learning has been widely explored and implemented in K–12 schools, and integrative curricula have more recently become popular in higher education. Much of what is taking place on campuses under the label of integrative learning is in the form of isolated projects and initiatives, in much the same way that learner-centered pedagogy appears in individual classrooms but not necessarily throughout a curriculum or institution. For example, in reporting on the research by the AAC&U in regard to trends and themes in integrative learning, DeZure, Babb, and Waldmann (2005) note that campuses do not use the language of integration consistently: "The phrase 'integrative learning' has limited common meaning. Even familiar concepts like learning community, capstone, first-year experience, general education, interdisciplinary (or variously, cross-disciplinary, multidisciplinary, or transdisciplinary) courses or studies have differing applications" (p. 24). Many of these approaches are implemented within highly structured curricula that are not integrative by design.

Klein (2005) examined the difference between the terms *interdisciplinary* and *integrative* and identified *integrative learning* as the umbrella term for "structures, strategies, and activities that bridge numerous divides such as high school and college, general education and the major, introductory and advanced levels, experiences inside and outside the classroom, theory and practice, and disciplines and fields" (p. 8). She defines interdisciplinary as a subset of integrative learning. Interdisciplinary studies maintain the separateness of the disciplines. They provide multiple perspectives on a common theme that, in the end, may not become fully integrated because of the competing discipline-specific ideology. Beane (1997) also cautioned that often multidisciplinary efforts are *mistakenly* referred to as integrative:

> As discussions about curriculum organization develop and labels multiply, a pretty reliable way to figure which is which is to check for the root word *discipline*, which refers to the differentiated categories of knowledge that subjects represent. Where that root word is used—multidisciplinary, interdisciplinary, cross-disciplinary, and so on—something other than curriculum integration, usually a realignment of the existing subject, is almost always intended. (p. 12)

The rise of "studies"—cultural studies, women's studies, popular culture studies, minority studies, urban studies, and so forth—has given alternative curriculum design visibility. These programs focus on a central theme, examining the theme or problem from multiple disciplinary lenses. They tend to include arts and sciences disciplines, such as psychology, sociology, humanities, literature, and philosophy. Although studies of this sort may be integrative, they are not de facto integrative simply because they have a theme. Wiggins and McTighe (2005) refer to the "twin sins of design," the first being the focus on coverage, which we have already discussed in regard to the focus on content. The second is theme-based activities. Wiggins and McTighe use the example of an elementary classroom unit on the theme of apples. Each teacher has students involved in various apple-related activities; no intellectual goals, however, are identified. There is no attempt to show students what was important—what the point is. There is just a theme tying the activities together. The same criticism applies at higher levels. Looking at a theme such as minority studies from multiple disciplinary perspectives does not ensure that there is integration.

When we refer to integrative design, we will use Beane's definition and refer to a curriculum that is structured to seek integration through pedagogical strategies as well as through overall curriculum design. The pedagogical strategies that we will propose in the next section represent three main areas in the new research on learning: community-building strategies, sharing power with students to develop learner autonomy, and ongoing assessment to monitor growth and to make learning an intentional activity. We agree with Beane that a learner-centered curriculum should be conceptualized as a set of occurrences, those occurrences being targeted types of learning (transformational, critical thinking, reflective thinking) as opposed to discipline content. And those occurrences need to be tied to the big ideas referred to by Wiggins and McTighe and to the desired outcomes.

In Chapter Five, we will look at college curricula that are organized around what we would argue are occurrences or experiences that all students share in common, at intervals in the curriculum. Each program that we use as an illustration begins with an orientation course that focuses on the unique features of the curriculum, a course that is meant to be transformative. We use *transformative* as Mezirow (1991) uses it to characterize learning experiences that change a person's beliefs and transform the person's original perspective or understanding. Transformative learning asks individuals to assess the contexts by which they know things and question their assumptions.

A course that fosters transformative learning employs specific strategies. The first is what Mezirow (1991) referred to as an activating event, which can involve the presentation of either a disorienting dilemma or conflicting evidence for the student to resolve, some exercise or problem that challenges the students' habitual way of knowing or understanding. This event is followed by the students' critically examining the underlying assumptions underpinning that habitual understanding. Critical discourse and reflection are part of this examination and are followed by an opportunity to explore or test out new conceptions.

The idea of disorientation is critical to a postmodern view of curriculum, for the postmodern world is not a stable, single reality but a result of myriad interpretations. Doll (1993) called for curriculum with just the "right amount of indeterminacy, anomaly, inefficiency, chaos, disequilibrium, dissipation, lived experience" (p. 176). A postmodern constructivist curriculum recognizes this indeterminacy of reality and seeks integration. The design of the curriculum acknowledges the multiple layers of meaning and the individual learners' construction of meaning, asking individuals to integrate their prior learning and prior understanding and to use it in a variety of contexts.

What We Mean by Learner-Centered

We have used Doll's characteristics of postmodern curriculum as the organizing principles or general framework on which to create a new curriculum. When we talk about learner-centered theory, we will refer to specific pedagogical strategies in terms of placing those strategies within a curriculum framework so that they achieve a desired effect: community building, power sharing to foster learner autonomy, and ongoing assessment for continuous improvement.

Learner-centeredness as we have been describing it is actually a blending of two visions of curriculum design, both constructivist by nature. The first vision is considered student-centered. Schiro (2008) explained that this ideology places the needs and concerns of the individual learner, rather than the academic discipline, at the center. Educators espousing this ideology focus on learning environments with a central focus on how to organize instructional materials in order to maximize the growth of the learner. "Curriculum is not thought of as subject-matter-set-out-to-be-learned but rather as environments or units in which people can make meaning" (p. 10).

The second vision as defined by Schiro (2008) is that of the social reconstructionists who believe that education can solve society's problems. According to Schiro, "Social Reconstructionists assume that education ... of individuals in appropriately revitalized schools can lead to social transformation" (p. 134). Pedagogy in this view emphasizes peer interaction, social relevance of material, problem solving, and collaboration.

The major difference between the two visions or ideologies is more a matter of emphasis: social reconstructionists accuse student-centeredness of being too self-absorbed, too focused on the individual rather than preparing students for their social responsibility. Our view is more generally postmodern or constructivist, encompassing both the student-centered and social reconstructionist visions. We will use the term *learner-centered* to encompass this broader view of the constructivist approach to curriculum design that focuses on types of learning and learning environments, strategically placed within a curriculum framework, thus creating coherence and fostering integration.

The American Psychological Association (APA, 2008) integrated theory and research from psychology and education to define fourteen learner-centered principles—psychological factors that have an impact on learning. The principles are constructivist in approach. They take into account motivational and affective factors as well as developmental mental and social factors and individual differences. McCombs (2001) summarizes the research on learning, focusing on the APA principles, and concludes that "research shows that learner- or person-centered systems can improve learning and motivation by meeting students' needs for belonging, control, and competence" (p. 192). As we have noted previously, we define learner-centered practices in three domains: (1) creation of community, (2) sharing of power, and (3) use of assessment for continuous improvement.

Community

Community building is a key component of a learner-centered curriculum. Community is essential if students are going to learn from one another, collaborate, feel safe to experiment, and be prepared for a workplace that is increasingly more team based. One of the recommendations made by Bruffee (1995) in developing a postmodern curriculum is to have students explore the number and variety of communities to which they belong and also to explore the relationship between their existing communities and the discipline they are choosing to enter.

> The goal would be to help students understand their academic studies—of mathematics, chemistry, sociology, English, whatever—as re-acculturation, and specifically as re-acculturation into communities in which knowledge is a construct of the community's constituting language or form of discourse. Along with this basic expertise in the working of language and other symbolic systems, furthermore, would necessarily go basic expertise in how people live and work well together. (Bruffee, 1995, p. 26)

The focus on students' understanding that they are already part of multiple communities is important because it broadens their concept of what community means, helps them recognize multiple communities that can intersect with one another, and begins to establish a sense of previous knowledge on which they can draw.

It also provides an opportunity for students to begin broadening their sense of what learning is, where it takes place, and the degree to which activities outside the classroom are interrelated with those inside the classroom. Bransford, Brown, and Cocking (2000) describe learner-centered classroom environments as places that promote intellectual camaraderie through such activities as collaborative problem solving and other group activities that involve active learning. They note that cooperation in solving problems and argumentation among classmates enhance cognitive development. Other well-established means of creating community include learning communities, freshman year experiences, group service components, team projects, and capstone experiences. These strategies also foster integrative learning.

Power and Control

In Chapter One, we discussed the role of sharing power in the fostering of creativity and motivation, noting that the three factors that lead to better performance are autonomy, mastery, and purpose. To reiterate here, motivated learning requires individuals to feel free to make choices in the process, believe the activity has value, and decide they can conquer the challenge.

There is typically little power sharing in curriculum design. As we noted in the previous chapter, curriculum is most often linear. It is a sequence designed by the discipline authorities, and it is handed to students as a prescription to follow. Students begin with entry-level courses and proceed to more advanced courses in a designated sequence. They have few options in either the selection or combination of courses.

Admittedly, some subject material depends on prerequisites. A student's success in chemistry often depends on the prerequisite math, and success in biochemistry depends on the prerequisite chemistry. However, even minor opportunities for choice seem monumental to students who have never shared any power at all. A colleague described to us the way program coordinators at his institution selected general education offerings for students and called them "directed electives," an oxymoron betraying the constricted nature of the curriculum and the insistence on maintaining power and control on the part of the program coordinators. A learner-centered curriculum would build in as much choice, negotiation, and self-direction as possible.

An equally compelling reason for increasing students' opportunities for choice is related to their beliefs about success and failure. Research in this area, also referred to as attribution theory, examines how people explain why things happen. Do they take personal responsibility, or do they blame an external force? Svinicki (2004) explains,

> The best strategy for attribution retraining is to put the learners in a situation in which they have to make choices and experience the consequences of those choices. If the instructor or some other force outside the students is always calling the shots and telling them what to do and how to do it, when thing go wrong, students are very justified in pointing the finger at the instructor. (p. 163)

Related to this is the phenomenon of learned helplessness, characterized by learners' simply giving up because they have no control. As Svinicki explains, "They 'learned' that they were helpless, and that situation then expanded to the rest of their functioning" (p. 164). Empowering learners fosters the development of learner autonomy, which, as we said earlier, is one goal of a learner-centered curriculum.

Choice is a key feature of learner-centered pedagogy. Learner-centered practices offer learners control over their learning and create a sense of relevance to learning tasks, thus supporting motivation. Learner-centered pedagogy fosters the sharing of power between students and teachers, offering students choices and responsibility, and contextualizes learning to increase the sense of relevance—both of which serve to create intrinsic motivation for learning and to create learning environments that are conducive to creativity. Learner-centered curricula will do the same. In the following chapter, we will show how different programs increased students' opportunities for choice.

Assessment

When we talk about assessment of curriculum, we are talking about two functions of assessment. First, we will use assessment as the basis for the design of the curriculum; second, we will look at assessment as an ongoing process for monitoring the progress of students' learning as they work through the curriculum.

Fink (2003) and Wiggins and McTighe (2005) both advocate a "backward" approach to design, Fink in looking at individual course design, and Wiggins and McTighe in looking at both course and program design. This backward approach simply represents the shift in thinking that we make when we shift into the learner-centered paradigm and focus on learning outcomes. In other words, we begin at the end or, to use the language of Wiggins and McTighe, with the *desired results*. Just as teachers identify specific learning outcomes students should be able to demonstrate by the end of their class, curriculum designers identify the learning outcomes students should be able to demonstrate at the completion of the program. And therein may lie the most difficult task. In Chapter Two, we asserted that many accrediting bodies have made significant changes in order to shift the emphasis of review to student learning. As we will see in Chapter Six, having an accrediting body that outlines the learning outcomes can make programmatic revision much easier or can at least streamline the process, because the parties then only have to work out the evidence that they will need in order to be able to determine that the outcomes have been met and then plan the learning experiences that will get the students to that point.

Unlike professional and technical schools, traditional academic disciplines generally do not have clearly delineated outcomes. The knowledge and skills needed to perform as a pharmacist are more obvious than the knowledge and skills of a graduate from a bachelor's program in the liberal arts. In a report published by the AAC&U, the National Leadership Council for Liberal Education and America's Promise (2007) identified five key educational outcomes that should serve as the foundation of a quality education. Those outcomes are (1) strong analytical, communication, quantitative, and information skills; (2) deep understanding of and hands-on experience with the inquiry practices of disciplines that explore the natural, social, and cultural realms; (3) intercultural knowledge and collaborative problem-solving skills; (4) a proactive sense of responsibility for individual, civic, and social choices; and (5) habits of mind that foster integrative thinking and the ability to transfer skills and knowledge from one setting to another.

We began Chapter One with similar calls for stronger liberal arts preparation, but as many of us have experienced, assessing general education is often difficult and fraught with political issues. Nonetheless, statements like that of the National Leadership Council, along with discipline-specific outcomes, serve as the starting point for design. Using Wiggins and McTighe's model (2005) of backward design, the next step would be to determine the acceptable evidence: What will be the means for assessing student competency? Having answered this question, we would follow with planning the experiences and instruction. Wiggins and McTighe put this very succinctly: "The rubber meets the road with assessment.... Agreement on needed evidence of learning leads to greater curricular coherence and more reliable evaluation by teachers" (p. 19).

Carefully constructed ongoing assessments are essential to a learner-centered curriculum. Teacher-to-student assessments are the mechanisms used by individual teachers to see if learning is taking place. Student-to-teacher assessments are the feedback students give to teachers about their learning and about whether the designed learning environment is having the intended effect. Peer assessment provides a valuable opportunity for students to compare their understanding with others and to try to understand another's frame of reference. Self-assessment in this curriculum design is also an essential component. Reflection and revisiting one's knowledge and understanding foster self-regulation.

Schön (1983) emphasized the role of reflection in the learning process. In writing about Schön's work, Scott (2008) noted that Schön, like Bruner (1996), called for a curriculum that was an "interactive process of assimilation, with the capacity of the human agent to reflect on what they receive from their environment and in the process change it" (p. 115). Schön argued for the need for both problem setting and problem solving. Problem setting involves seeing the contextual influences of one's choices. He wrote, "In real-world practice, problems do not present themselves to the practitioner as givens. They must be constructed from the materials of problematic situations which are puzzling, troubling and uncertain" (pp. 39–40). In Chapter Five, we will show how self-assessment and reflection are built into curricula and how online tools can be an asset to this process.

Wiggins and McTighe (2005) make the point that understanding is about transfer. We've used a number of terms to describe this. Deep learning and seeing from multiple contexts are other ways of talking about transfer, the ability to use knowledge in new configurations and new contexts, to transfer it from one situation to another. Wiggins and McTighe write,

> The challenge is to make it [transfer] more likely by design rather than by luck or by natural disposition. With deliberate and explicit instruction in how to transfer (and assessments that constantly demand such transfer), the learner must take what were initially bits of knowledge with no clear structure or power and come to see them as part of a larger, more meaningful and more useful system. (p. 43)

Assessments that ask students to transfer are those that ask students to extract information and apply it. Assessments should avoid focusing on facts and repeating information as it was presented. As Wiggins and McTighe point out, there's a difference between knowing the right answer and *understanding*. Carefully crafted assessments will be able to reveal that difference. Chapter Six will provide an in-depth look at a variety of assessment mechanisms.

Chapter Summary

In this chapter, we have presented a framework for curriculum design that challenges long-standing assumptions about curriculum as seen through the lens of the instructional paradigm. In developing this framework, we have relied on Doll's postmodern, constructivist theory of curriculum, and we adopted the four characteristics he uses to characterize a constructivist curriculum: richness, relations, recursion, and rigor. We chose his theory because it meshes well with the research on learning that supports learner-centered pedagogy. We have organized that research into three overarching areas: community, sharing power, and assessment. The learner-centered curriculum focuses on the individual's process of learning to become an autonomous learner, yielding the added benefit of fostering creativity.

4

Leading Curricular
Implementation

Curricular change of any kind is a challenge. How many of us have initiated a curriculum change based on what we believed to be necessary for meeting the needs of students, only to have our proposal denied or what we perceived to be the potential benefits negotiated away during the curricular review process? Curricular change toward learner-centeredness does not promise to be any easier. It is perhaps even more challenging, for it asks for change that doesn't fit the current system; it's outside the paradigm. Implementing curricula that depart from the norm will require vision, creativity, and tenacity on the part of those leading the change. In this chapter, we will discuss some strategies for implementation, recognizing that curricular change toward a fully learner-centered design may take place incrementally as members of one's institution continue to deepen their understanding of learner-centered principles.

Adopting a Rogerian Approach

Implementation is really about persuasion, and, in looking at this process, we would like to adopt a postmodern approach to persuasion that differs considerably from traditional argumentation. Traditional argument is typically a win-or-lose proposition in which the person presents an arsenal of information, data, statistics, and other rhetorical appeals, attempting to overwhelm the opponent in order to win. With its emphasis on hierarchy (winning or losing) and on a single, dominating point of view, this approach aligns with the values of the instructional paradigm. If we are to be truly learner-centered in our practices, then our approach to implementation should reflect the values of the new paradigm.

Young, Becker, and Pike (1974) adapted the work of Carl Rogers to create a new form of argument, not surprisingly called Rogerian argument. Rogers (1980) believed in multiple realities, a very postmodern concept, and he posited that no one could know anything except through his or her own perceptions.

> I, and many others, have come to a new realization. It is this: The only reality I can possibly know is the world as I perceive and experience it at this moment. The only reality you can possibly know is the world as you perceive and experience it at this moment. And the only certainty is that those perceived realities are different. There are as many "real worlds" as there are people! This creates a most burdensome dilemma, one never before experienced in history. (Rogers, 1980, p. 102)

In this postmodern view, the goal of persuasion is not to win but rather to come to understand, to recognize the multiple perceptions of different individuals in order to find common ground on which to build consensus.

For Rogers, the discussion that ensues carries more importance than the outcome, a view that sounds remarkably like Doll's description of curriculum, one in which learning results from repeated discussion in order to come to an understanding. Persuasion in this view is about learning and about broadening and deepening one's understanding. Our strategy for implementation, then, will focus on those discussions and on developing an ever-deepening understanding of learner-centered principles.

Before we look at the possible discussions that can take place to deepen the understanding of learner-centered curriculum, we need to address a key element of Rogerian argument: reduction of threat. Rogers posited that when an individual feels threatened, he or she cannot respond in any other way but to defend himself or herself. Young et al. (1974) explain that the theory of Rogerian argument

> rests on the assumption that out of a need to pre-serve the stability of his image, a person will refuse to consider alternatives that he feels are threatening, and hence, that *changing a person's image depends on eliminating this sense of threat.* Much of men's resistance to logical argument seems explainable by this assumption. A strong sense of threat may render the reader immune to even the most carefully reasoned and well-supported argument. (p. 274)

In Chapter One, we discussed this same point in relation to Svinicki's work (2004) on the role that individual beliefs play in one's willingness to accept conceptual change. She emphasizes that prior learning can inhibit student learning and that in the face of evidence, students will resist new concepts unless the change in understanding is somehow profitable to them. For new ideas to be accepted, they need to be perceived as better than the old and benefiting the individual in some way. Without the sense of personal gain, people perceive new concepts as threatening.

So as we embark on the process of implementing curricular change, we must consider how to reduce the sense of threat that learner-centered curricula may pose. We know that many of the principles associated with learner-centered pedagogy can be threatening to faculty. For example, our discussions of the concept of sharing power with students have been met, more often than not, with resistance and skepticism. Similarly, making the case that assessment is key to fostering learning is oftentimes hampered by aggressive institutional postures regarding the need for assessment as a means of defense against public perceptions of the quality of graduates. Given these existing positions, it is likely that suggesting that we revise our curricula to be more flexible and accommodating to individual differences and less rigid in regard to academic discipline will also be met with resistance. How, then, can we reduce the threat that is often associated with change and begin the discussions that bring about consensus?

Reducing Threat with Programs That Fit: Compatibility

Two terms used repeatedly by researchers on curricular change to determine the success of innovative programming are *compatibility* and *profitability*. Compatibility is seen as the degree to which the program fits the norms, values, and goals of the institution, the culture. Profitability refers to the gain individuals will experience as a result of making a change. These two terms align with two main strategies that are employed in Rogerian rhetoric: first, reducing the audience's sense of threat, and second, finding commonality on which to build a shared bridge of information. In the case of curriculum revision, all parties generally share these two goals—the first, enhancing one's institutional culture, and the second, gaining something from the change.

According to Rogerian rhetoric, the first step toward reducing threat is for the persuader to show that he or she understands the audience's position and finds merit in it. Various studies have reported on the implementation process of curricular change (Levine, 1980; Kliewer, 1999; Smith et al., 2000; Yearwood, Singleton, Feldman, & Colombraro, 2001; Colley, 2009), emphasizing the need to understand and respect the institutional or college culture. Understanding culture is part of showing that one understands the opposition's worldview.

Burkhardt (2006) offers interesting insight into institutional culture in relation to innovative programming in an article examining the rise and fall of Arizona International College (AIC). AIC was an innovative interdisciplinary experimental public liberal arts college overseen by the Arizona Board of Regents. It was created and implemented within two years, which might seem to herald the agility that higher education seeks to develop in being responsive to workforce or population trends; however, the speed with which the college was developed was so far outside the norms of the university governance system that it violated the culture. The goal was for AIC to become an independent institution within the Arizona system, but initially it was housed within Arizona University (AU). This created what Burkhardt referred to as "uncertain institutional space" (p. 160). Exacerbating the hesitancy that AU faculty had in regard to this college that was created outside their own governance system, the regents "decreed that AIU [later the name was changed to AIC] would hire faculty on long-term contracts rather than tenure" (p. 160). Burkhardt noted, "AIC was perceived, for example, as an effort to undo tenure in the state system generally, to offer an 'unapproved' curriculum lacking in (disciplinary) rigor and to undermine UA faculty governance and the (disciplinary) legitimacy of other UA programs" (p. 162). In short, the effort was seen as a clear threat to the culture of academe.

The Ferris State University bachelor of integrative studies (BIS), which we will introduce in the next chapter, is an example of how cultural compatibility enables successful implementation. Tierney (1995) states that we cannot consider curricula divorced from the context in which they are situated. The BIS program is situated in a career-focused university where the emphasis has been on employability upon graduation. The university was founded for the purpose of retraining displaced lumberjacks 125 years ago, when the lumber industry in Michigan collapsed. The focus on jobs has been consistent since that time. When the BIS was initially presented, it was designed for people already in the workforce who either needed to complete a degree in order to be promoted or who needed to redirect their skills in order to move within their current place of employment. This focus on jobs and employability resonated well with the faculty and the administration during the curricular approval process. The BIS, for example, received far less resistance than did the proposal for BA majors intended as preparation for graduate school, because for many, graduate school did not constitute employment upon graduation.

The BIS was implemented at an interesting juncture, a time when the Michigan economy made it necessary for many adults to return to the university to reinvent themselves. Both returning adult learners and traditional-age students are faced with a challenging future where jobs and the workforce in general are changing rapidly. It is difficult to make any guarantees to anyone regarding future employability because the landscape continues to change. Rather than training students for a job in a society that some people say is becoming "dejobbed," the BIS emphasizes the demonstration of talents and abilities, multiple skills, and adaptability, along with the ability to learn and transfer skills to new contexts. The BIS program is in many ways a return to the original mission of the university as articulated by the founder, but designed for workers in a new century in an entirely new economy and social reality.

Martsolf et al. (1999) also emphasize the need to respect institutional culture and offer two additional cautions regarding curricular change: (1) the project must be voluntary, and (2) administrative support and resources are essential. Colley's study of curricular implementation echoed these findings:

> The findings suggest that implementation is positively impacted by faculty belief in the philosophy, availability of resources, and previous knowledge and experience. Results also suggest such factors as lack of time, implementation in isolation and minimal group interaction related to the implementation negatively impact the process. (2009, p. 179)

The caution that the project must be voluntary is also relevant to the notion of reducing threat. If faculty members are not voluntarily involved, the project is simply doomed. Understanding this need for voluntary participation, we then must ask, *How does one gain buy-in and support of the project?* First of all, if a group of supporters can be identified, it is best to have them try to engage their colleagues in order to generate enthusiasm and additional support. Faculty who are already using learner-centered practices in their classes might be the most likely to want to experiment with learner-centered curriculum design. As both Martsolf et al.'s and Colley's studies indicate, implementation cannot occur without strong faculty leadership, by individuals who are accepted, trusted, and respected and who can rally collegial support. These individuals need to articulate educational objectives and herald the benefits of change.

Reducing Threat Through Profitability

Profitability, the degree to which the program benefits the campus, is another key factor for successful implementation. In the example of the BIS implementation, the new program was perceived as a profitable addition to the curriculum. The description of the degree emphasized that individuals' programs could not replicate any existing programs. This statement alleviated the threat that often accompanies new curriculum proposals. Further, faculty members immediately recognized the opportunity that the degree offered to individuals who, as working adults, had very specific objectives in terms of what they needed to learn and who otherwise might not be able to find a good match with existing programs. The program also promised to become a recruiting tool for students who had left the university without completing their bachelor's and entered the workforce, but now needed or wanted a degree in hand. A further benefit was its potential for retaining students on wait-lists (usually up to two years) for two-year applied associate degree programs in the College of Allied Health. The BIS offered them the opportunity to gain a bachelor's degree and remain engaged with the university while waiting for their specific career focus in allied health. Further, it served as a means of retaining students who could not find the program that suited them: it enabled them to build multiple skill sets; and, because in building individual programs, students often use existing minors and certificates, it proved profitable across campus as a program that increased other program minors. So the benefits to the campus were many.

In regard to interdisciplinary program implementation, Burkhardt (2006) suggests that

> administrators should invest time and resources in reconfiguring the discursive terrain of the institution through engagement and translation not only upwards to central administration and outward to the rest of the institution, but also internally to the faculty within the interdisciplinary unit. (p. 166)

We especially like his use of the word "translation" because we will use the metaphor of language learning to frame specific strategies later in this chapter. Administrators need to take care to ensure that they translate—in other words, that they try to help all parties come to understand one another.

O'Banion's *A Learning College for the 21st Century* (1997) features the lessons learned by five community colleges that made a successful transition to a learner-centered culture. Each one emphasized the role of leadership and the need for dialogue. Maricopa College began its journey by taking part in a Pew Higher Education roundtable, which emphasized the need for true dialogue. Elsner (1997), reporting on the Maricopa experience, writes,

> In a college committed to learning, dialogue is an essential but often neglected skill. Maricopa actually began a series of training and facilitation efforts to assist and inspire its members to communicate in meaningful

dialogues. One of the major problems in higher education is that policy leaders, faculty and staff in many of
our institutions do not know how to talk to one another.
The language of the CEO is embedded with references
to control, competition, and protection of territory. The
CEO is often a primary barrier to open communication,
to real talking, real sharing and real exchange. (p. 170)

Attention to language is an essential part of becoming self-aware
and intentional in our actions, a point we will return to later in
this chapter.

In the case of Maricopa, the support of leadership extended
to the governing board. The governing board replaced its routine
business with a series of strategic conversations on significant
topics, conversations run by faculty, staff, students.

As a result of Maricopa's emphasis on helping leaders
learn and learners lead, several hundred staff members
have become qualified in group process and communication skills to facilitate discussion. This outcome is one
of the characteristics of the desired learning paradigm in
which we learn from one another. (Elsner, 1997, p. 176)

Profitability can also take the form of incentives, which play
an important role in stimulating change. This is where accrediting
bodies can sometimes help, as we mentioned in Chapter Two. In
the case of many of the PharmD revisions, the looming threat
of the accreditation visit coupled with stories from other campuses
where the visits had already taken place created a climate of instant
volunteerism. The change in accreditation standards functioned as
a trigger event, an event that O'Banion (1997) defines as a kind
of teachable moment or "an event that releases energy and creates
opportunity, an event that leaders can use to focus thought and to
rally troops to action" (p. 227).

Having faculty and administrators visit other programs that have been successfully implemented provides a further incentive. Colleagues can generate enthusiasm and also provide useful feedback regarding potential pitfalls. The trip itself can be a bonding experience, a time for colleagues to get out of the regular routine and focus on the possibilities of the task at hand.

In their description of the Palomar College transition to a learner-centered culture, Boggs and Michael (1997) discussed the importance of external validation. The most notable external validation came from the often cited Barr and Tagg article (1995) in *Change* magazine. In addition, however, the college president wrote several articles for national publications, and staff members made numerous presentations and held two national videoconferences on the subject of the learner-centered campus. "Faculty and staff members who attend conferences are frequently asked by colleagues from other colleges about the innovations at Palomar. When they return, they are not only proud of what is being accomplished at Palomar, but they are even more committed to the paradigm shift" (Boggs & Michael, p. 196).

Carrots are always useful. One provost offered individual programs incentive funds if they successfully reduced credits in the major to a certain level. Suddenly there was renewed interest in hours to graduation on that campus. The same method could be used for learner-centered curricula. Other incentives could be technology support or classroom renovation funding to support the initiative. In our experience, when classroom renovation and technology support are offered as possibilities, interest grows. Renovation of physical spaces can be a very effective way to generate energy and enthusiasm for pedagogical reform. If this is the case, and we believe it is, then coupling renovation with curricular reform makes a lot of sense. We will address this issue in greater depth in Chapter Eight.

Both compatibility and profitability must be present for success. Burkhardt (2006) explains: "Strategic engagement and translation must operate at the cultural or symbolic level and the economic or structural level both internally and externally in order for the innovation to be owned as compatible and profitable within the larger institution" (p. 165). Put more simply, people support what they help build. They need to take ownership and remain invested and engaged. It is the role of leadership to keep communication open and transparent in order to foster a trust in the innovation and a belief that it will contribute to the well-being of the existing structure. Further, leaders must take actions that are congruent with learner-centered principles and when possible make symbolic gestures that demonstrate support and belief in the process.

Preparing Faculty

In her report on several learner-centered curriculum reform initiatives in professional programs across the United States, Jones (2002) emphasizes that faculty preparation is essential. Learning opportunities and chances to explore new ideas help build confidence in the implementation plan. Faculty need time to explore and experiment. She writes,

> In successful curriculum reform, change agents have thoughtfully planned and developed a series of ongoing faculty development activities. These initiatives are designed to help faculty conceptualize their new ideas and to receive constructive feedback from their peers regarding suggestions for improvement. (p. 81)

The curriculum changes that Jones describes were focused on pedagogical changes. The reforms centered on faculty adopting new learner-centered strategies in their classrooms. The actual structural design of the curricula was not affected in these cases, and as we have argued, learner-centered pedagogy alone does not constitute a learner-centered curriculum design.

We need to make this distinction clear before embarking on a discussion of implementation. For a curriculum to be learner-centered, learner-centered pedagogy within individual classes is needed along with a curriculum design that places those courses in a learner-centered context or framework. Faculty development, therefore, demands a two-pronged approach. The first effort—which should probably precede the other—is to focus on faculty adoption of learner-centered pedagogy and course design. There are numerous ways to do this, many successful strategies coordinated through faculty centers, and good books to guide the process. Some widely used titles include

Learner-Centered Teaching: Five Key Changes in Practice (Weimer, 2002)

Inspired College Teaching (Weimer, 2010)

Creating Significant Learning Experiences: An Integrated Approach to Designing College Classes (Fink, 2003)

Applying the Science of Learning to University Teaching and Beyond (Hackel, 2002)

Developing Learner-Centered Teaching: A Practical Guide for Faculty (Blumberg, 2008)

Helping Students Learn in a Learner-Centered Environment: A Guide to Teaching in Higher Education (Doyle, 2008)

The Professional Organizational Development (POD) Network (www.podnetwork.org) is also a useful resource, providing workshops, conferences, consultants, and other resources for faculty development.

The second faculty development effort must focus on curriculum design in regard to programs and majors. It is this facet of faculty development that we will address. In *Leading the Learner-Centered Campus* (Harris & Cullen, 2010), we made the case that there are four steps to shifting institutional processes, such as the curriculum process, to a learner-centered focus. The first step is to analyze the current process in order to understand how it is a product of the instructional paradigm. That was our aim in Chapter Two. The second step requires analyzing what the new process would look like if governed by learner-centered principles. That was our aim in Chapter Three. The third and fourth steps ask leaders to model best practices and to infuse the process with assessment. We will focus on these two final steps in the remainder of this chapter.

When we say "model best practices," we mean that leaders need to adopt learner-centered attitudes and behaviors in their own roles in order to demonstrate the way. We will first consider some basic attitudes necessary in breaking down the divisiveness of the process itself and remaining open to experimentation. We made the point earlier that in a Rogerian approach to persuasion, ongoing conversation is essential, for through those conversations, individuals come to understand each other more clearly and become open to new ideas. We will suggest some specific discussions to consider as you embark on redesigning programs. These are framed as *What if?* conversations.

Adopting Learner-Centered Attitudes and Behaviors

In our examination of the curricular process in Chapter Two, we noted that traditionally there is a type of dual gatekeeping model to the curriculum development process. The term *gatekeeping* itself suggests stopping or preventing; it does not convey the idea of individuals at each level of review interpreting their role as one of contributing. In the traditional model, faculty members develop programs based on their discipline expertise, and the approval process begins in a unit or department and travels up through the college to a university-wide curriculum committee, with final faculty approval coming from the academic senate. Along the way, faculty give input, send proposals back to the originators for reconsideration, and eventually approve the program if it has met all the guidelines mandated by the academic senate and the registrar. At each level—the department, the college, and the division—an administrator also reviews the proposal with an eye on implementation, staffing, cost, marketing, and so on. If the resources are available and the program seems viable, the program will receive the seal of approval on its route through this channel. Once it has been vetted by the faculty and administration, it may require approval at a state level, where competing universities review the proposal to see if it seems worthy. This process reflects the hierarchical and competitive character of the instructional paradigm.

Although we would argue, and did so in Chapter Two, that this process typically overemphasizes territory, budget, and marketing at the expense of student learning, in truth it is unlikely that the process itself will soon be changed. The concept of dual gatekeeping, however, does not have to suggest a separation or divide between faculty and administration but rather a division of labor. A learner-centered approach will ask academic leaders to recognize this distinction rather than allow the dual gatekeeping to become divisive. By applying principles of Rogerian rhetoric to this process, it can become one of negotiation rather than one of winning or losing.

In Chapter One and at the beginning of this chapter, we looked at the factors that foster innovation and creativity, one of which was seeing things from multiple perspectives. If curricular review were approached as a process involving multiple perspectives, it would be more like a continuous improvement model, exemplified by the Higher Learning Commission's Academic Quality Improvement Process (AQIP), whereby reviewers act more like consultants than gatekeepers. When an institution is reviewed according to the AQIP, no single perspective determines the final outcome. Rather, the review relies on a continuous examination from multiple perspectives (action project reviews, portfolio reviews, site visits, and so on). The perspectives of the various reviewers are taken as a whole. Ideally, curriculum review could become a team process whereby each party is reviewing with an intent to improve rather than to prevent.

In Chapter Three, we emphasized that a learner-centered curriculum fosters community, is empowering, and is rich in assessment, and that the focus shifts from discipline content to learning environments. Leaders can do many things to improve learning environments and to add to curricular proposals from this vantage point. There are numerous proven strategies for developing community and engaging students. Freshman interest groups (FIGs), linked courses, learning communities, and service learning are just some of the strategies that are typically employed. To implement these requires administrative support in terms of both financial resources and logistics and scheduling. But perhaps even more important is for leaders to be knowledgeable about these strategies, to be enthusiastic about innovation, and to encourage creative efforts in curriculum design.

Three colleagues in different departments had an idea and approached their department heads about creating a learning community for gender studies that would link courses in humanities, social sciences, and literature. The English department head did not know if he could support it. Because he maintained a policy of cutting courses with low enrollment, he wondered how students would be recruited for the classes. He said he would have to ask the dean. The social sciences department head responded that she could not break the scheduling matrix, so she really could not see how to schedule it; in addition, the professor would have to teach it as an overload because she was already scheduled for a full load the following semester. The humanities department head said, "We've needed something like that! Let me see what I can do to make this happen"; she then proceeded to work through the necessary red tape to overcome issues with scheduling and found an ideal space on campus where the courses could meet both separately and as an entire group for guest lectures and discussion. She also provided the professors with a student assistant to help with developing materials and recruiting students for the course. As leaders, we can either pave the way and support change or we can explain that innovation doesn't fit our way of doing things. Learner-centered leaders do the former. Likewise, some administrators wrap themselves up in policies so that they can be protected from making decisions. To return to the physical space analogy we made in the Preface, leaders need to be in the business of taking down the walls.

As we noted, once leaders examine the process according to the instructional paradigm and then consider what the process would look like in a learner-centered paradigm, the next phase is for leaders to consider how to be more learner-centered in supporting curriculum revision, how to model the way. Here we would like to consider how research on innovation and creativity might inform this process.

In Chapter One, we identified four strategies that characterize an innovative mind-set: embracing the belief that intelligence is expandable, seeing from multiple perspectives, adopting a positive attitude toward failure, and maintaining a drive to succeed; and we discussed strategies that teachers can use in their classrooms to create environments that foster creativity and innovation. Leaders can employ these same strategies at the institutional level.

We referred to Langer's definition of mindfulness (1989): the ability to create new categories and maintain an openness to new information. One way to achieve this is for teachers to avoid presenting information as if it were the only possibility. In the example we just used of the three department heads, the English head and the social sciences head both responded in habitual ways, as if there were only one way to conceive of a course, a schedule of courses, and a staff for them. The humanities head, however, was open to seeing something new, trying to conceive of scheduling from a new perspective.

A colleague who is the director of a school of nursing and who has been working to implement learner-centered curricular revision in her school serves as a good example. She made numerous gestures to show her support. First, and perhaps most important, she attended all the faculty development sessions so that she was working in concert with her faculty to achieve the goal of a learner-centered curriculum. She revised the form she used for reviewing faculty so as to incorporate learner-centered practices, and she provided resources to her faculty in the form of books and conference participation. Her role as teammate, using the lessons from the development sessions and adapting those lessons to her own role, serves as a positive example of learner-centered leadership.

How we respond to failure or setbacks also becomes indicative of a creative and innovative mind-set. Tolerance for failure is critical if leaders are to create an environment that fosters inno-vation. One all too typical type of setback is budget cutting. As institutions struggle with financial stability and ever-growing costs, they periodically face mandated budget cuts. Rather than seeing the budget reduction process as a negative and thus beginning the process with the attitude that they are going to lose something, innovators use these times as opportunities to foster change. An illustration of these contrasting attitudes took place a number of years ago during a statewide recession. Two state universities faced the same issue; one took the doom-and-gloom approach. Programs were slated to be cut, the process was secretive, and the list of program cuts was announced on television by the university president, while faculty and students sat anxiously waiting to hear if their program was on the chopping block. Down the road, a sister institution took an entirely different approach and rolled out a public relations campaign describing their lean, agile approach to this budget challenge. Their enrollment actually flourished as a response to this public relations move, whereas students began fleeing the other university.

In writing about Lane Community College's transition toward learner-centeredness, Moskus (1997) noted the importance of creating a climate of trust. He used an example of a staff member who championed the idea of using the play *Oleanna* as a learning experience instead of holding the traditional opening-day events for the school year. The play triggered mixed responses. In spite of this, the staff member was awarded the college's first "risk-taker award" and was treated with respect by all parties. Moskus writes,

> The lesson learned is that it is important to create a climate of trust in which people can lead and fail without recrimination. The learning college cannot exist in a cautious, careful, fearful college community. A learning community supports risk-takers and rewards grand failures as well as grand successes. (p. 163)

Another critical factor in creating learning environments that are motivating and supportive of innovation is sharing power. When people are given the opportunity to make decisions for themselves, they are by nature more vested in the outcomes, and this contributes to an individual's willingness to persist. We quoted Amabile (1996) and made particular note that it is not a question of whether to engage in an activity but of being allowed to determine how to engage in the activity. Adopting behaviors that are learner-centered simply requires leadership to be mindful of the three domains of learner-centered research and practice: establishing community, sharing power, and monitoring assessment. Each of the recommendations made in the next section relates to one of those domains.

Engaging in Conversations About the Possibilities: What If?

In trying to think about curriculum from the perspective of the learner-centered paradigm, we have made the case that we need to try to set aside our preconceptions and become keenly attuned to those unexamined attitudes or realities that we have taken as fact. That will be the focus of our development strategy. We like to use the analogy of language learning when thinking about shifting paradigms. The instructional paradigm is our first language. We learned our first language naturally, somewhat unconsciously. We intuitively developed and accepted the structures that underpin it, and know it and use it with great facility even though we may not be able to articulate the grammatical rules. Talking about paradigms as languages can be a very useful metaphor.

We learn new languages through a very intentional, self-conscious process, paying conscious attention to the grammatical structure of the new language and applying that structure through continued practice. In the beginning, we use our first language as a point of reference and comparison. Eventually, after continued practice and as our understanding of the new language deepens, we no longer translate; instead, we eventually begin to think in the new language. For us to learn to speak in the new paradigm, we will have to remain always conscious of the new underlying structures that will guide our development, and consciously practice thinking and operating according to the new rules. We will make comparisons to the old paradigm and recognize the ways in which the new paradigm deviates from our habitual thinking. Eventually, after time and practice, we will no longer translate. We will think in the new paradigm.

We propose a set of questions for leaders to use in opening the discussion of learner-centered curricular review. These questions should stimulate thinking from a learner-centered perspective and help individuals become self-conscious so as to jump-start thinking in the language of the new paradigm.

Part of learning a new language is learning new vocabulary. When we become attentive to the language that we use, we begin to see underlying attitudes and beliefs. Our word choice is indicative of our belief system, cultural background, and sensitivity to issues of race, gender, religion, and more. As we venture into a new paradigm, we will gain a heightened sensitivity to the vocabulary of the paradigm.

Changes in language and vocabulary document cultural changes. For example, whereas it was once highly controversial for women to challenge the use of *he* as the universal pronoun, it is now part of standard textbook guidelines for avoiding sexist language. Similar lexical changes have taken place in regard to racial groups, as in the transformation from *negro* and *colored* to *African American* and from *black* to *people of color*, and in the shift from *crippled* to *handicapped* or from *disabled* to *physically challenged*. Even though some of these changes have ignited social debate about whether attention to language is somehow a totalitarian plot, those who understand language change know that such change is inevitable and not really controllable, although efforts to bring certain attitudes to the forefront of people's thinking can perhaps stimulate change. For example, it wasn't the attention to terms like *lady doctor* and *male nurse* that led to the disuse of these terms, but rather a societal shift whereby more and more women became doctors and more and more men became nurses, so the idea of a lady doctor or male nurse did not seem to be an oddity.

Schaefer and Zygmont (2003) commented on the adoption of learner-centered vocabulary in a study of nursing faculty teaching styles. They noted that "faculty may know the language of student-centered teaching but do not understand the language. As a result, they make statements that reveal dissonance in their philosophies of teaching-learning" (p. 241). For example, they may talk about sharing power with students but then adopt classroom policies or make statements about other pedagogical strategies that reveal an inconsistency in their understanding of what it really means to share power. In the transition between paradigms, the first issue we might consider is our language, and we might ask if there are terms that we are accustomed to using that suggest a "norm" that we are challenging.

In describing the transition to a learner-centered culture at Palomar College, Boggs and Michael (1997) wrote, "Language is important in American society. College leaders need to be sure they are saying what they intend to say" (p. 205). At Palomar, the process of transition began with a review of all documents—the catalogue, schedule, job descriptions, recruitment brochures, and all publications—to ensure that the language reflected a learner-centered focus. So, as part of our implementation scheme, we ask: *What new facets of the paradigm may require new vocabulary, and how could a change in vocabulary bring learner-centered principles to conscious attention?*

What If We Call It Something Else?

Let's begin with the most fundamental vocabulary item. What if we didn't use the word *curriculum*? The history of the term is very interesting, particularly in relation to the examination of curriculum in the instructional paradigm. The Latin word *curriculum* literally meant a racecourse or a chariot for running on a racecourse. Doll (2002) provides an overview of the history of the word that he claims is tied closely to Calvinism as well as to Ramos's taxonomy of knowledge. Ramos devised a hierarchical ordering of all knowledge in a linear, unbroken progression that Doll claims was denounced by colleagues because it diluted the importance of dialogue in the search for truth. A key point that he emphasizes is that Ramos thought he had categorized not only all knowledge but also the structure of acquiring that knowledge. Calvinists chose the word curriculum because it offered an ordered and disciplined way to steer their youth, to keep them on course. Doll writes,

> My reason for citing this history of the period between 1550 and 1650 is to help us appreciate the need for control which virtually all thinkers felt at the time. . . . Curriculum, then, as a method to bring control and order to life goes back much farther than America's twentieth-century industrialization, where it is often placed. (p. 34)

So, considering the historical use of the term and its association with control, what if we used a different word?

What if we used the term *academic plan* rather than curriculum? Lattuca and Stark's definition of an academic plan (2009) aligns with a learner-centered approach. The conscious choice to "rename" curriculum is an important point in regard to rethinking our approach to curriculum design and review. The academic plan as defined by Lattuca and Stark is organized around "critical decision points" that enhance the overall learning experience. Their use of "plan," rather than curriculum, is intentional, as plans have purposes, implied evaluation, and adjustment. The idea of identifying critical decision points also reflects the idea of "play" or flexibility within a curriculum, allowing for student choice and engagement. We like the term academic plan both for the reasons Lattuca and Stark articulated and also as one simple way to heighten awareness and bring attention to a new way of conceiving of an idea. The word also conjures the well-known saying, *The best-laid plans of mice and men often go awry.* In this way, use of the word *plan* suggests a recognition of the possibility of failure and represents an openness to risk-taking and an acceptance or tolerance of error.

What If We Rethink Prerequisites?

What if we were to rethink our language in regard to the word *prerequisite*? Prerequisites are typically indicated in one of three ways, by specifying (1) courses that should have been completed prior to enrolling, (2) a certain number of credits that should have been completed, or (3) permission of the instructor or department. The idea of prerequisites should ensure that a student has the needed background or skills to succeed in a course. Sometimes the rationale for prerequisites, however, gets separated from student learning. In a recent proposal before an academic senate, a program coordinator asked to remove prerequisites for a course, RELG 400. The prerequisites had included the following courses: RELG 250, RELG 310, RELG 320, and ENGL 200. The reason given for changing the prerequisites was that requiring three religion classes and an English class was hurting enrollment. This begs the question, what is it that a student learns in those previous courses that is necessary for taking the course (RELG 400), and if only one course is sufficient in addition to ENGL 200, why were three listed in the first place? Was that an effort to increase enrollment in the other courses? Where is the discussion of student learning in this episode? Here is an excellent opportunity for leaders to bring student learning to the forefront of decision making by simply asking the question, How does the proposed change affect student learning?

How might we change the way we word prerequisites to avoid these kinds of issues? For example, prior to taking English 250, students must achieve a grade of C or better in English 150. If rather than focusing on the grade and the course we were to focus on specific learning outcomes, as identified in the course, students and faculty might experience a shift in thinking. How would students' attitudes toward entering English 250 change if the prerequisite were stated something like, "Prior to taking English 250, students must demonstrate in a portfolio of no fewer than thirty pages their ability to write to multiple audiences at varying levels of style and to develop a clear thesis supported by evidence, incorporating secondary sources and demonstrating rhetorical and grammatical competence"? A statement of this sort might shift the emphasis from grades to student ability and demonstration of it. Making this change would not be all that impractical because many English departments, for example, already use a portfolio assessment component. The statement of prerequisite would simply describe what is already happening but change the traditional language. So perhaps rather than talking about prerequisites for courses, we could talk about *demonstrated competencies*.

What If We Rewrite Course Descriptions?

Course descriptions are an important part of curriculum development. Traditionally the course description focuses on content to be
covered. In describing the five key changes in practice associated
with a learner-centered approach, Weimer (2002) referred to a shift
in thinking about the role of content. Rather than focusing on the
amount of material that needs to be covered—or, in the language
we have used previously in describing the instructional paradigm,
the dissemination of a quantity of knowledge—teachers are asked
to consider more broadly the learning outcomes of the student.
Weimer recommends thinking about content first as a vehicle
to develop learning skills, second as a way to promote students'
self-awareness of their learning, and third as a way to use content to
involve students: "Let us resolve to stop 'covering' content and
start 'using' it to accomplish learner-centered objectives" (p. 71).

Take, for example, the following course description:

> ARTH 203: An introduction to visual art—sculpture,
> painting, drawings, pottery, textiles—produced by
> African Americans from the colonial era to the present.
> Attention will be given to the aesthetic links between
> African art forms and African American artistic
> expression.

Consider the following revision that focuses on learning
outcomes:

> ARTH 203: In this Web-enhanced course, students will
> develop the ability to interpret selected works as a part
> of a culture and to justify those interpretations, demon-
> strating an understanding of the interpretive process.
> By looking at works or historical events from multiple
> perspectives, students will gain an increased under-
> standing of the techniques and methodology of the
> discipline. Through interactive lecture discussion and
> both synchronous and asynchronous online discussion,

students will explore key cultural and historical themes
as well as aesthetic issues.

What if course descriptions no longer described what the student
will get in the course but focused rather on what the student will do?
Written in this way, the course description shifts from a description
of what information the student will receive to a description of what
the student will demonstrate. The revised version also provides
some indication of the learning environment.

As we design our curriculum, what if we focused on course aims
and experiences rather than on descriptions of content? We might
gain a clearer focus on the student learning outcomes as well as on
learning environments that could foster the achievement of those
outcomes. Thinking about our course descriptions in this way also
begs the question of why a course is important to the curriculum.
The course aims should make that answer evident.

What If We Focus on Structure?

When we learn a new language, we have to focus on its structure.
In fact, many people who study foreign languages will admit that
it was in learning the second language that they came to understand the grammar of their first one. The structure of curriculum in
the instructional paradigm is linear and additive. Curriculum in the
learner-centered paradigm is recursive and reflexive. The curriculum planner, then, will want to consider ways in which a curriculum
can be structured to achieve this recursivity and reflexivity.

We have quoted Bruffee (1995), who said that curriculum
should be designed around a set of occurrences. In many regards,
the examples we will offer in the following chapter do just that.
Rather than focusing exclusively on the content, reformers focus on
the student's interaction with content and on how active learning
strategies could complement and enhance that interaction. The
Quest University curriculum, which we will examine in more
depth in Chapter Five, does this. The curriculum design at Quest
focuses on several key occurrences: the orientation to the program,
the student's question, the academic plan for years three and

four, the study away experience, and the capstone project. These experiences create the structure of the curriculum. The rest is fairly open and up to the choice of the student. This path of occurrences provides enough structure to guide students but allows them enough play to direct their own interests and to integrate the experiences.

What If We Downplay Credit Hours?

Challenging devotion to the credit hour may be the most radical and most difficult change to achieve. We made the point in Chapter Two that the credit hour is the coin of the realm, used to determine everything from the cost of a course to the load of a faculty member to the completion of a degree. In writing about the Carnegie Unit, O'Banion (1997) states that it is "but the tip of a very large iceberg that has frozen education into a structure created for an earlier social order" (p. 8). He goes on to quote Patricia Cross, who concluded that it is the commitment to time-defined structures that stands in the way of progress. O'Banion sums up by saying, "This inherited architecture of education places great limits on a system struggling to redefine and transform itself into a more learning-centered operation" (p. 9). The credit hour is such a fundamental unit that it seems almost impossible even to discuss a change in thinking. We quoted Tagg (2003), who made the assertion that in the instructional paradigm, time is the constant, and learning is the variable. Our goal is to make learning the constant, and time, maybe, more variable.

If nothing else, we can try to catch ourselves when we fall into habitual thinking about credit hours. For example, in the curriculum development process, is it really essential to parcel out course content according to the amount of time devoted to it? Accrediting boards no longer require detailed accounting of the time taken to deliver information; they have made the shift toward student learning outcomes and continuous improvement through assessment, yet this practice remains in place at many institutions.

Can we become more flexible in regard to student credit hours toward degrees, make transfer from program to program less of a penalty, and promote ease of transfer from one institution to another? If we can resist the urge to add credits to majors and instead integrate coursework, we will be making a shift toward learner-centeredness in our curriculum process. In Chapter Seven, we will also consider the ways in which technology can be used to make class time and subsequently credit hours more flexible.

Making the Most of Timing

The adage, timing is everything, is very true. In the case of accrediting boards' changes to standards, the external force not only makes the timing right but also drives the process in a timely manner. Other opportunities also can affect timing. The opportunity to renovate physical facilities is a perfect time to make academic renovations and allow the academic needs to influence the architectural choices.

The greatest challenge for faculty is finding time to work together on curriculum issues. Simply altering scheduling to make it easier for faculty to meet can facilitate the process, and leaders never suffer when they respect the time constraints of others. Recognizing the time limitations and workload of others is a matter of respect, and people naturally respond favorably when others pay them respect.

Infusing Assessment

Because of the importance of assessment to learner-centered pedagogy and principles, we will devote Chapter Six to various types of both classroom and programmatic assessment. Our discussion here will focus on the role of assessment in the implementation process. Earlier we made the pronouncement that the implementation process is doomed without voluntary faculty involvement. The same is true for the role of assessment. Learner-centered pedagogy, curriculum, and institutional mission are all predicated on assessment. In other words, you cannot be focused on student learning if you are not checking to see if learning is taking place. And this brings us back to the reduction of threat through compatibility and profitability.

Compatibility: Creating a Culture of Assessment

When we talked about compatibility earlier in this chapter, we referred to the degree to which the program fits the institutional culture. In terms of using assessment to drive implementation, we are talking about developing a culture of assessment—creating an institutional environment that values assessment practices and results, and uses results to inform decision making. When asked about the role of leadership in assessment, Trudy Banta, an international authority on assessment, responded, "The first thing for an academic administrator to do is to make it plain that they value data" (Kelly, 2009). In other words, data are highly regarded and *used*, not just collected. Perhaps most important, assessment should be the response to an ongoing and genuine curiosity about student learning.

There is probably no more important task for leadership than to create a culture of assessment. What do we really mean when we say a "culture of assessment"? At some institutions, this phrase has come to mean that assessment is ongoing and transparent. We would argue that a true culture of assessment is much more than the presence of ongoing assessment on a campus.

Throughout the previous chapters, we have made reference to Dweck's theory of intelligence, which distinguishes between an incremental view of intelligence and an entity view, or, as she characterized it in a more popularized version of her work, the growth mind-set versus the fixed. The person with a growth mind-set believes that mistakes are opportunities to grow and learn, whereas someone with a fixed mind-set is obsessed with good performance and therefore rarely takes risks. We discussed the need for teachers to create an environment where it is safe to make mistakes. If we are to successfully infuse assessment in order to drive curricular change, or change of any sort, we need to adopt a growth mind-set.

Our experiences as AQIP reviewers, as attendees at conferences on assessment, and as administrators overseeing accreditation reviews lead us to believe that the most fundamental problem with assessment in higher education today resides in the fixed mind-set of the participants. Too many times, assessment is approached as a means of proving one's worth rather than as an opportunity for growth. We have served on numerous reviews where institutions have generated mountains of data, sometimes seeming to intend to overwhelm the reviewers with tables and numbers, but haven't analyzed or used the data. Like the learner with a fixed mind-set, their purpose is to prove that they are meeting performance standards. If they do expose some areas of deficiency, they offer explanations rather than identifying the area as an opportunity for growth.

Rather than thinking of assessment as a kind of test that we either pass or fail, we would do better to think of it like an annual trip to the doctor. Even though we may feel fine, if we are concerned with preserving our health, we routinely have check-ups to monitor what medical professionals believe to be symptoms of good health. If a blood test, for example, reveals that we have abnormally low potassium, our typical response is not to ignore it or to remind the doctor that our cholesterol level looked really good. Rather, we consider why it might be low and what actions we can take to raise it to a normal level, because our goal is to improve our health. This is the attitude we need to develop if we are to have a true culture of assessment, and leaders have the capacity to make this happen.

Profitability: Adding Value to Assessment

In order to foster a culture of assessment and reduce the sense of threat that assessment can often create, leaders need to make assessment data valuable. If proposals for projects are data driven and actions are taken as a direct response to data collected, then collecting data becomes valuable. A friend who directs a writing center recounted the story of when, twenty-five years ago, she proposed to her dean that funding be allocated for a writing center to serve students across the curriculum. The dean said that he had to have data to prove the need. At first she was incensed and thought that the response was just a stalling tactic on his part, but because she wanted to get the project funded, she pulled together a team to conduct the university's first large-scale writing assessment project. The results more than supported the need for a writing center, and the project was funded. A bonus was the grassroots interest in writing across the curriculum that resulted from the assessment project; an added bonus was the sense of accomplishment felt by the faculty involved in the project, which led to a long-term commitment to large-scale writing assessment in her department. This one simple request for data had long-ranging effects and stimulated an interest in assessment that became part of the department culture.

Just as a teacher in a classroom can create an environment conducive to risk-taking and developing a growth mind-set, leaders can do the same on an institutional level. It is the responsibility of leadership to ensure that truth is more important than results. If participants fear program closure or other kinds of retribution for poor assessment results, then they will never adopt a growth mind-set toward assessment. One way to create an environment conducive to risk-taking is to develop a system of rewards for continuous improvement. If assessment results reveal a shortcoming, focus not on the shortcoming but on the measures that were taken to address it and the success of those actions. In Chapter One, we talked about the need for teachers to foster autonomy; one way was to focus on the student's individual progress toward outcomes rather than comparing students to one another. This same technique can be applied to assessment: rather than focusing on comparing program to program, focus on the individual program in relation to its own progress.

Another strategy we discussed in Chapter One in regard to combating what Svinicki (2004) called "the illusion of comprehension" was to ask students to use information rather than simply identify it. We can apply this same principle to assessment. Instead of having them simply report on findings, ask those responsible for assessment to do something with those findings, to transfer the results to a new context in order to fully examine them. Many of the standard measures that get reported are not direct measures of student learning but indirect measures like freshman year retention rates or six-year graduation rates. These measures, though, can be the trigger for more focused direct assessment. As in the example of the blood test indicating low potassium, the one assessment can then function as a trigger for future direct assessments that can explain the results of the initial assessment. If the six-year graduation rate is good, how does it relate to other data, such as employer satisfaction, alumni surveys, capstone assessments, and so on?

Earlier in this chapter, in discussing Palomar College, we noted the importance of gaining external validation for program implementation. This is also a great strategy for creating a culture of assessment. Faculty involved in assessment should be encouraged to share their results at conferences and through publication, and leaders should do the same. External validation can fire internal enthusiasm and a sense of worth and accomplishment. Support for faculty to share assessment practices is money well spent. The long-term commitment to writing assessment referred to in the previous example was to a great degree fueled by teams of faculty members reporting on assessment projects at national conferences.

Chapter Summary

In this chapter, we suggested that leaders approach the implementation process using the rhetorical strategies espoused by Young et al. (1974) in their Rogerian argument, a technique based on Carl Rogers's postmodern conception of the individual's sense of reality. In doing so, we offered strategies for reducing threat to individuals and establishing shared values on which consensus can be built. Drawing on the concept of learning as a result of conversation as presented by both Rogers and Doll, we offered a series of *What if?* questions for leaders to use in opening the conversation on curricular reform. Using the analogy of learning a new language, we suggested that leaders model innovative and creative approaches to curriculum by challenging norms, and always keep student learning at the heart of any discussion of curriculum. The act of considering new vocabulary has the promise of opening an entirely new way of discussing curriculum and maintaining a focus on intentionality as we work through the process.

5

Learner-Centered Design
in Practice

In *Leading the Learner-Centered Campus* (Harris & Cullen, 2010), we introduced a matrix designed to determine the degree of learner-centeredness in teaching practices within a department or unit. The Syllabus Assessment Matrix can be used by either a department head or chair to assess the degree of learner-centeredness as a starting point for planning faculty development or by individuals interested in assessing their syllabus.

In Table 5.1 we offer a similar tool designed to be used either in assessing a current program or as a guide in program development. The Syllabus Assessment Matrix identified three main categories, the three domains of learner-centeredness we discussed in Chapter Three: community, sharing power, and assessment. We will use those three categories again, but add the four elements identified by Doll (1993): recursion, rigor, richness, and relations, recognizing that there is a certain amount of overlap among these criteria.

Just as some courses are more learner-centered than others, some curriculum designs are more learner-centered than others. We have organized this chapter around the criteria of the rubric of design elements and describe some different illustrative programs that have incorporated these learner-centered design elements to one degree or another. We conclude the chapter with a speculative revision of a history major and consider the questions that might guide the revision process.

Table 5.1. Rubric for Evaluating Curricular Design

Design Element	Description of Design Element	Low	Medium	High
Recursion	Provides nonlinear elements; revisits main concepts			
Rigor	Offers opportunities for integrative learning; is organized around problems or issues rather than strictly discipline content; includes integrative learning strategies, inquiry skills, communication, critical thinking, problem solving, and so on			
Richness	Incorporates transformative experiences into design; includes synthesis of deep learning strategies: performances, projects, portfolios, critical thinking, self-assessment, reflection, practical application			
Relations	Provides for transfer of knowledge between and among contexts; includes capstone and culminating experiences			
Community building	Provides opportunities for collaboration, team building, service learning, and active learning; supports and encourages cooperation and collaboration			
Power sharing	Provides opportunities for student input and choice in academic plan; provides multiple avenues for students to demonstrate competencies			
Assessment	Is based on learning outcomes; includes assessments throughout curriculum; provides assessments that ask students to apply knowledge in varying contexts; emphasizes that assessment is a major component of teaching			

We have chosen five curricula that we believe illustrate learner-centered design to varying degrees. The first two models are professional doctoral programs in pharmacy (PharmD), one at Ferris State University (FSU) in Michigan, and the other at Western University (WesternU) in California. We chose these two because they offer a comparison along the continuum of learner-centered design. They are both designed in response to changes made by their accrediting body, the Accreditation Council for Pharmacy Education, and one program (WesternU) served as a model for the other (FSU). We also use two examples of bachelor's degrees in integrative studies, one from Miami University in Ohio and the other from FSU. The fifth example is Quest University in Canada, a new university curriculum designed to foster integrative thinking. We would like to emphasize that our focus is on the structural design of the curriculum rather than on the content. In Chapter Three, we discussed the role of content in the curriculum and quoted Wiggins and McTighe as well as others cautioning that rather than focusing on content to be covered, curriculum design needs to emphasize larger goals, essential questions, and key performance tasks, which become the blueprint for design.

Recursion

Recursion refers to the spiraling nature of design called for by Doll and others. Traditionally we have conceived of curriculum as a process of adding new knowledge through a succession of courses or experiences. From a learner-centered perspective, we will design a curriculum that is nonlinear, one that offers students opportunities to repeat, review, and reconsider their understanding of concepts and ideas. Admittedly, even in a linear curriculum, a student revisits concepts as he or she becomes more knowledgeable, and ideas are revisited in different courses. A curriculum that is recursive by design, though, builds the opportunities for revisiting and reassessing one's understanding into the academic plan rather than leaving it up to chance.

Some programs use a block design in order to achieve recursion. The PharmD at WesternU is an example of an innovative curriculum based on a block system of learning. In each block in the WesternU program, students learn through lecture, group work, discussion, student presentations, peer learning, and other teaching activities. Block topics are organized according to disease states, so, for example, one block will be devoted to cardiovascular issues. Within that block, then, students study the relevant anatomy and physiology, biochemistry, drug therapies, and so on, gaining a multidimensional perspective of the system. When the next disease state is introduced, students revisit the study of anatomy and physiology, biochemistry, and drug therapies in relation to the new topic.

Quest University also uses a block design for its university curriculum. The first two years, called the foundation program, are configured in a block system borrowed from Colorado College. The Quest program has sixteen blocks of foundational courses. (See Figure 5.1.) Students take each course one at a time in three-and-a-half-week blocks. According to Quest's Web site, the foundation program intends to

- Provide a breadth of knowledge about the world and our place in it

- Offer an integrated approach to learning

- Expose the student to the most important academic subject matter in the arts and sciences

- Help students become aware of present-day issues and future possibilities in these subjects

- Create an intimate educational experience by ensuring close contact between students and teachers

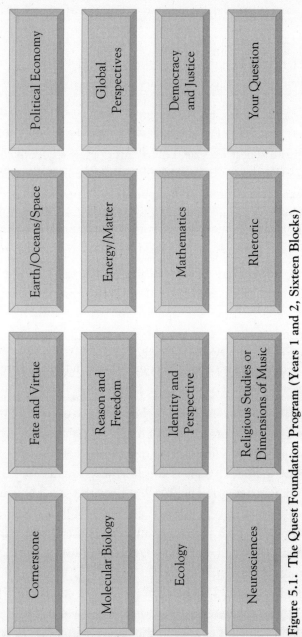

Figure 5.1. The Quest Foundation Program (Years 1 and 2, Sixteen Blocks)

- Foster global citizenship by focusing on issues and events with international consequences

- Ensure greater intercultural communicative competence by helping students learn a variety of perspectives on contemporary academic topics

The three anchoring blocks are Cornerstone, Rhetoric, and Question. The Cornerstone class is the first class, a sort of orientation to the Quest experience. In this course, students come to understand the intensive one-block-at-a-time curriculum model as well as experience the multidisciplinary and integrative approach of a Quest education. The course also serves as a model for inquiry-based learning.

The second block is Rhetoric and directly follows the Cornerstone. Regardless of the theme of the course, the Rhetoric block is designed to introduce students to rhetoric across the curriculum at Quest, giving them the opportunity to work intensively on good writing and on effective public speaking, which will be an expectation of every course in the curriculum.

The Question block comes at the end of the two-year foundation experience. In this block, students build their academic plan with the help of an adviser and develop their research question. Students generate a two-page proposal, which may be a statement, question, or set of questions. Some sample questions students have studied in the past include "What is the best way to educate a child?" "What is a just foreign policy?" "What are the social obstructions to public health in developing nations?" and "What is honor?" The Question proposal is a significant element of the Quest education, and a considerable amount of energy and enthusiasm pervades the campus during the Question block.

Miami University's bachelor of integrative studies (BIS) seeks recursion through strategically placed courses within the academic plan. Like the anchor courses in the Quest plan, Miami's program uses three integrative seminar courses that serve as transitional experiences in the progression of coursework. The first is an introduction to integrative studies in which the emphasis is on self. Students examine options within the degree and create a personal statement of educational objectives. They work on self-reflection and assessment skills as well.

The second seminar shifts the emphasis from self to others. The key component of this seminar is a service learning experience. Students examine their relationship to the larger community and begin to integrate concepts they have learned in their coursework to that point. The third seminar is focused on product. It is a capstone culminating experience requiring students to produce and present a project.

The BIS at FSU is also recursive in design. The orientation to the program requires students to build their academic plan. Rather than focusing on an entry point that students build on in a steady progression to an end point, this nonlinear plan asks students to pull together multiple knowledge sources and tie them together. It is analogous to creating a collage with a theme that emerges from the interplay of the parts. Discovering the commonalities and interplay among their various areas of content knowledge becomes the students' challenge. In Chapter Three we quoted Bernstein, who wrote that integrative design combines one's vertical knowledge (knowledge gained through school) with one's horizontal knowledge (knowledge gained through one's life travels), or as Beane labeled it, integration of experience with knowledge. The design of the program is based on this intersection of horizontal and vertical knowledge and the recursive assessment of that knowledge.

Rigor

In calling for rigor in curriculum, Doll referred to flexibility, for curriculum to be to some degree self-organizing. We have interpreted this concept of rigor as integrative design, programs that

involve students in the choice and selection of content. Some of
the features that characterize integrative learning include intentional focus on critical thinking, communication, and problem
solving.

Miami's BIS is a program specifically designed for students who
have an associate degree or have completed other college-level
work. The BIS program allows students to build a bachelor's degree
that meets their needs.

In addition to the general education requirements for the university, students choose two concentrations. These form the integrative
foundation for the program. Concentration I is chosen from a list
of ten:

Applied Kinesiology   Applied Sociology
Contemporary American   Cross Cultural Leadership
Experience   Families, Gender and Society
Environmental Studies   Information Technology Strategy
Geographic Information   for Organizations
Science   Understanding Media and Visual
Organizational Leadership   Culture

Students can also choose a self-designed concentration. Concentration II is a three-course plan derived either from the primary list
of concentrations or from the Miami Plan Thematic Sequence.

Similarly, the BIS at FSU asks students to focus on multiple
capacities that they wish to develop and combine for individualized
career paths. Although each self-styled program is different, the
orientation and capstone experiences and general education core
create commonality. Regardless of concentrations, minors, and
associate degrees that are combined to create the individual's
program of study, the culminating experience requires students (1)
to demonstrate exceptional skills in communication, presentation,
and self-assessment in order to meet programmatic goals intended
to foster learner autonomy, and (2) to market themselves in their

chosen career path. In recognition of the changing demands of the twenty-first-century workforce and the need for lifelong learning, students are additionally required to plan for ongoing professional development.

In 2007, the FSU PharmD curriculum was revised with the specific intention of integrating coursework. The result was three new integrated courses. The first new course, called Pharmacotherapeutics, integrated the former courses in diagnostics, pathophysiology, and therapeutics and added pharmacokinetics, which represented new content in the curriculum. Another new course was called Drug Action, which resulted from the integration of pharmacology and medicinal chemistry. A third new course on infectious diseases resulted from the integration of microbiology, chemotherapeutics, and pharmacotherapeutics.

Coursework in the first and second professional years focuses on basic sciences, including biochemistry, pathophysiology of disease, pharmaceutics, pharmacology, and medicinal chemistry, as well as practice management. Progressively more integrative coursework is presented to students in an attempt to predispose them to cross-discipline application of information and problem solving. Third-year professional coursework centers on therapeutics and integrated patient case studies, with additional content in pharmacy practice management, drug literature evaluation and research methods, sociopharmacy, and pharmacy law.

Richness

Doll defined richness as education that asks students to examine multiple layers of meaning and interpretation of experience. We interpret his explanation of richness to mean experiences that foster deep learning; we characterize deep learning as a student's ability to transfer knowledge into new contexts and to apply knowledge to different situations. The pedagogical strategies that facilitate deep learning include discussion with peers, reflective writing, practical application, and reading. Active learning combined with self-assessment and reflection characterize teaching strategies for deep learning.

Curriculum designs that build in reflection, practical application, and active learning experiences are rich in design. The revised FSU PharmD includes increased experiential learning early in the program. The program carefully designed practice skills labs to run concurrently with didactic material—which is presented in team-taught lectures—as well as introductory and advanced pharmacy practice experiences. Practice skills labs provide both an active learning environment as well as a setting in which patient and prescription simulations can be presented to students. As students progress through the program, they gain experiences in internal medicine, ambulatory care, community pharmacy, and institutional pharmacy. The professional growth and development plan includes a student code of conduct, progressive dress code policy, and support of professional student organizations and fraternities. The design integrates the necessary scientific foundational content with community-based experiential learning, leading to direct patient-based practicum.

The WesternU PharmD is likewise rich in experiential learning. From the beginning, experiential learning is included. In the early clinical experiences, students are assigned their first "rotation" in either a community or hospital pharmacy. During their last year and a half, students work one to two four-hour days a week plus an eight-hour weekend day in several settings, including hospitals, chain and independent pharmacies, and compounding sites. Students also take part in team case assignments and presentations. These tasks require students to transform lecture material into a case-based format, formulating disease-specific patient scenarios from the information. Faculty and peers review students on these assignments. Evidence-based medicine team project assignments call for students to critically search for and assess an article on a specified topic and then take part in what program faculty call a Journal Club discussion.

Quest University requires a service learning experience of their graduates. One to four blocks constitute experiential learning opportunities; two blocks, study of a nonnative language; and three to six blocks, free upper division–level electives. According to Quest's Web site,

> The main focus of the concentration program is depth of understanding—sustained attention to a question of personal importance to the student. Attaining a measure of depth means knowing what a good question is, and knowing how to pursue the answer to it. It is a skill for life, and a preeminent achievement of a liberal arts and sciences education at Quest.

This description of the third- and fourth-year curriculum highlights some of the key learner-centered principles. First is depth of understanding, or as we described earlier, a curriculum that is deep rather than broad. Second is the importance of relevance. Students choose a question that is of personal importance and are thus more personally motivated to discover the answer.

Relations

Doll described relations in terms of wholeness. In earlier chapters, we made reference to the fragmentation that can sometimes characterize the undergraduate experience. Universities keep struggling to help students connect the various facets of their academic programming—for example, the relationship among general education courses, program major and minor courses, and cocurricular learning experiences. Learner-centered curriculum design addresses this sense of fragmentation. We made the claim in the previous chapter that the learner-centered curriculum takes into account the complex, idiosyncratic, and personal nature of learning.

One way that curriculum designers have addressed the personal nature of learning is by building in opportunities for reflection. Quest University, for example, has reflective assessments embedded in the Capstone block, including a retrospective letter to one's freshman self and a prospective letter to one's self five years hence.

The FSU PharmD instituted a reflective journal that is part of its ongoing program assessment. Each year, students are asked to reflect on their progress toward becoming a professional. Likewise, reflection is a key component of the WesternU PharmD. Students report that reflection allows them to gain a deep understanding of content through the reevaluation of content that is built into the program.

The Miami University BIS integrative learning seminars provide the "set of occurrences" that characterizes the learner-centered curriculum. These seminars require self-assessment and reflection, and their design creates learning environments that move the student from focusing on the self to focusing on the community and others. Likewise, the FSU BIS incorporates reflective assignments in the orientation and capstone experiences, which become part of the student's program portfolio.

Community

Community is a key feature of learner-centered practice. In a learner-centered curriculum, students become part of a community and come to recognize their membership in various communities. The learner-centered classroom community fosters collaboration, learning from one another, and supporting one another in the process of learning. We've made the point several times that learner-centered creative environments are those that are intellectually challenging but that are also places where it is safe to make mistakes.

Both of the PharmD programs we have used as examples foster community through team building and collaborative projects. The ability to work in teams is an essential skill for anyone in a health profession, and from the very beginning of the program, students work with one another and with students in other health care professions in order to become accustomed to the collaborative nature of their profession.

At WesternU, students gain a variety of community-building opportunities through teamwork and collaboration in courses as well as in the clinical experiences that begin in their first year. One specific learning strategy, called the Post Lecture Assignments, are designed to evaluate students' ability to apply knowledge gained from reading and lecture and to use evidence-based medicine to respond to specific questions. Students must participate in teams in answering questions and presenting their results. The assignments are evaluated on both the completeness of the response and the presentation by the team. Students also take part in team case assignments. As one student commented,

> The most amazing thing about WesternU is that it truly is a community. When you apply to a program at WesternU, you are really applying to a big family. This will be even more apparent as the colleges become intertwined with each other—through the new Interprofessional Education Program—this is crucial for offering amazing patient care in the future.

The effectiveness of community building is not surprising, considering that the university was founded on the concept of intersecting science and compassion. It has extended the mission of a humanistic approach to science to its physical presence. WesternU's technologically state-of-the-art modern lecture halls, characterized by a distinctive hexagonal seating arrangement, allow for closer contact between lecturers and students, and spill-out spaces and rooms for teams to work can be found strategically located outside the lecture hall.

The president of WesternU also refers to a "visible sense of community" that students enjoy at the university. According to WesternU's Web site,

The institution's success is due to the emphasis placed on the education and preparation of interdisciplinary primary health care service teams. The University's educational philosophy focuses on the preparation of highly skilled health care professionals who are also compassionate, humanistic caregivers. Faculty, staff, students, administrators, alumni and supporters refer often to the "WesternU Family," reflecting the caring, nurturing campus environment.

The FSU BIS has a challenge when it comes to team building because each student has an individualized plan of study, so there are few opportunities for collaboration. In an attempt to meet that challenge, the orientation and capstone courses were designed as fully online experiences in which the students share the same course shell. This provides an opportunity for interaction between the two course groups. The students are also in an online advising course shell where assessment data are collected. In that course shell, a discussion board is open for students to share information about courses, internship opportunities, and other items of interest. Because the program enrolls a large number of adult learners, this means of interaction among students has been highly successful. The adults new to the program have met other adults with similar life paths and academic experiences, and they feel very comfortable sharing advice and past experiences with one another. The program also has a Facebook presence that serves as an opportunity to keep alum involved in the community and also share program successes with community members.

Power Sharing

In earlier chapters, we discussed power sharing in terms of allowing for options. Oftentimes students emerge from the K–12 experience having had little or no choice in regard to their education. Therefore, even minimal opportunities for students to make their own choices can seem monumental to them. In looking at curriculum design, we focused on opportunities for choice in courses or ways of fulfilling requirements. In the curricula that we have been using as examples, we see a variety of ways that faculty share power with students. The most restrictive in terms of student choice is the FSU PharmD. In fact, students actually lost elective credits as a result of the curriculum revision. The WesternU PharmD, however, has reasonable opportunities for students to share in power. WesternU has been able to build in sixteen credits of electives, offering students opportunity for choice and control over their academic plan.

The open design of the FSU BIS offers students a tremendous amount of control and autonomy. They create their own learning outcomes and their own program design with the assistance of the program coordinator. Some items are negotiated, and the majority of students have been very open to suggestion because many enter the program without crystal-clear program goals.

The Quest curriculum is very strong in power sharing. The student plan consists of four primary elements: (1) the question, (2) the course plan, (3) the reading list, and (4) the capstone project. The question is the student's chosen topic of inquiry, which can range from a very broad topic like "What is courage?" to something very specific like "How does U.S. foreign policy impact hunger in developing nations?" The course plan consists of a list of six blocks that will contribute to answering the question; elective blocks that might lend an interesting perspective; and at least one experiential learning opportunity, which might include service learning, study abroad, or an internship. The reading list is intended to provide students with a broad context for understanding their question. Students, in collaboration with their adviser, develop a reading list comprising at least five seminal works that relate to their question. A capstone project serves as the culmination of the curriculum. The project can take a variety of forms, ranging from a video production or presentation of a research paper to a work of creative writing or a poster presentation at a professional conference. Of equal importance to the content of the project is the presentation of the material. The Quest learning outcomes—critical thinking, personal development, social engagement, and preparation for lifelong learning—should be demonstrated in the capstone.

This description of the third- and fourth-year curriculum highlights some of the key learner-centered principles. Relevance is both a key to motivation and a feature of sharing power. Students choose a question that is of personal importance and are thus more personally motivated to discover the answer. They become highly engaged and empowered through opportunities to develop their own curriculum. It is highly integrative, interdisciplinary, and inclusive of multiple communities of knowledge. The emphasis on rhetoric across the curriculum and on individual guided research, along with the immersive course design, all function to foster learner autonomy and deep learning.

Assessment

We have asserted that carefully constructed ongoing assessments are essential to a learner-centered curriculum; and learner-centered design begins with learning outcomes and then works backward to determine the mechanisms that will be used to assess students' achievement of those outcomes. All the programs we have been referring to have learning outcomes, but the programs vary greatly in their choice of the means of measuring the achievement of those outcomes. The FSU PharmD, for example, has a robust automated assessment tracking program that monitors learning outcomes down to the course level. The program also captures assessment data from multiple perspectives. However, it relies heavily on indirect measures, a concern that the school is in the process of addressing.

The WesternU PharmD has multiple assessments, both direct and indirect, that are embedded into the program. In addition to the typical examinations and quizzes, the program employs an assessment method based on direct observation of students in a planned clinical encounter, called Objective Structured Clinical Examination. It also employs in-class assessments, which we will talk about in greater depth in Chapter Six. In short, these quick assessments provide instructors with immediate feedback regarding student learning.

In the FSU BIS, students begin the program with an initial assessment of their current knowledge based on prior learning and experience and produce a statement of philosophy that begins to integrate the various facets of their backgrounds. In Chapter Two, we discussed how in the instructional paradigm, students lose credits when moving between disciplines because individual disciplines do not value the credit hours from other disciplines. In contrast, no knowledge is discarded or discredited in the BIS; rather, students work to integrate all their knowledge from various sources. The philosophy statement is revised each semester as part of ongoing self-assessment. Each semester, students must also assess their progress toward meeting their individual learning outcomes based on new knowledge gained that semester. This ongoing assessment creates continuity and focus for the individual programs of study. The major programmatic assessment mechanism is a portfolio that is organized according to learning outcomes and students' demonstration of achievement of those stated outcomes.

Quest is a very new curriculum and as yet does not have many formal assessment mechanisms in place at the time of our writing. At this time, the most important assessment tool is an exit interview with all graduating seniors. Each interview is scripted and conducted by outside professionals. It is based roughly on the kind of survey that Light (2001) developed, asking students to describe their best teachers, best classes, the greatest impact on their social lives, and so on. Quest also has reflective assessments embedded in the Capstone block. For direct measures, the program administers a test on quantitative reasoning and problem-solving skills as part of the exit interview. Although the program is new and the assessment plan is still in development, it is already enjoying impressive results on the National Survey of Student Engagement, beating every other school on the continent!

Revising an Existing Program

Most of the examples we have referred to are programs that were newly constructed. Most of us, though, are in a position of revising an existing program rather than building one from the ground up. The rubric that we introduced at the beginning of this chapter (Table 5.1) can be used as a tool for revising an existing program. The first step would be to assess the current program for the degree of recursion, rigor, richness, and so on. Many existing programs already have, to one degree or another, some of the learner-centered features we have identified, but as we stated earlier, the presence of learner-centered features in individual classes does not ensure a learner-centered curriculum.

One of the challenges in revising an existing program is to resist the temptation to simply add new courses or requirements. As an example, we will look at a general history major. In addition to a foreign language requirement and general education courses, the major in this model history program requires thirty-six credit hours that are organized in categories. Students begin by choosing two 100-level survey courses in either American history or world history. Students are then directed to select three 200-level choices from a list of seven options. Then students choose three courses in American history at the 300 level and another three courses in world civilizations at the 300 level. All students take a capstone course, HIST 400: Research in History.

Because we are using a hypothetical example, we will give ourselves the advantage of having a group of program faculty who have been deepening their understanding of learner-centered practices in their individual classes and as a group have decided that they would like to apply the principles to the redesign of their program. The actual starting point for them will be to examine the learning outcomes for the program. The next step will be to develop a plan for how the achievement of those outcomes will be measured, as well as where and when. The learning outcomes should reflect the big ideas, to use the language of Wiggins and McTighe (2005). Rather than asking, What does an historian need to know? we want to ask, What can an historian do, and how can students demonstrate that understanding?

A good example of this kind of planning is Indiana University's History Learning Project (Diaz, Middendorf, Pace, & Shopkow, 2008). The curriculum overview lists seven typical components of any history course: (1) understanding the nature of the historical discipline and analysis, (2) dealing with primary sources, (3) dealing with secondary sources, (4) dealing with evidence in textbooks, (5) constructing and evaluating arguments, (6) conducting research, and (7) writing for history. Each of these components has learning outcomes by course level (100, 200, 300, 400) based on Bloom's Taxonomy: recognition and comprehension at the 100 level, interpreting and applying at the 200 level, explaining and evaluating at the 300 level, and, finally, creating at the 400 level. For each learning outcome, the History Learning Project identified operations commonly required for the component, accompanied by possible assessment examples.

The consideration of the program outcomes and their assessment will be followed by an examination of the current program using the rubric to brainstorm possible changes and specific strategies for meeting program outcomes. In the previous chapter, we offered some *What if?* questions to guide implementation, so here we offer some questions for our program faculty to think about as they consider ways to make the design of their program more learner-centered. First of all, what if the American history or world civilizations introductory courses served as an orientation to the program? What would be the large issues in regard to becoming an historian that could be addressed through the introductory survey courses? What key ideas could be presented that would be repeated in the upper-level American and world history courses? What experiences in the orientation would establish the foundation for the capstone in research? What assessments in the orientation can serve as a benchmark for end-of-program assessment?

A second consideration arises in regard to the list of 200-level options. The list is diverse: Michigan History, History of Sports, History of Medical-Health Care, History of Science-Technology, African American History, American Business History, and African American Cultural Experience. Within this list of options (which most likely arose from the special areas of interest of program faculty, along with general education courses for other colleges), what is the overarching learning outcome? What should students achieve by completion of the 200-level requirement? Are there commonalities among these courses that could be presented to students so that they had a clear sense of outcomes? Are there any opportunities for integration? Are there specific hands-on experiences or service learning opportunities that could enrich these experiences?

A third consideration is the interplay of general education and the major. Students' choices for general education courses will vary, but the general education outcomes should be common to all. How do those outcomes enhance the history major's understanding of history as a discipline? Where in the history curriculum can this be addressed? What if, for example, students were presented with the question, Where does the history major belong, in humanities or in social sciences—and why? History departments are typically housed in one of these two disciplinary areas. Considering that students are studying both humanities and social sciences for general education, why not bring those general education outcomes to bear on the identification of history as a major?

Another consideration has to do with developing community as well as developing rigor. Would it be a valuable trade-off to reduce the number of free choices in 300-level American history and world civilizations courses to incorporate a required integrated course in American history and one in world civilizations?

In the current model for the program, the program assessment falls at the end in the capstone. If one or two other required integrated courses were included, what assessments could be embedded? Are there other opportunities for assessing student progress earlier on in the program? In Chapter Seven, we will discuss the use of technology to get around some of the barriers that may stand in the way. Online tools can foster community and also assist in collecting assessment data.

Revising a program takes a lot of time, thought, discussion, and reflection. It is probably wise to approach the revision in stages, making incremental changes and measuring their effects. Program revision is an ongoing process guided by assessment results. We want to emphasize again here that like all the changes we have recommended regarding learning environments, program changes should be made in an environment where mistakes are acknowledged and used for improvement, an atmosphere conducive to creativity and learning.

Chapter Summary

In this chapter, we have offered some examples of learner-centered curricular design in practice. As we noted at the outset, these examples fall along a continuum between instruction-centered and learner-centered design. Regardless of the degree to which these designs achieve their goals, each focuses on the process of students becoming autonomous learners and takes into account individual differences among learners. Reflection and revision of one's understanding are common to each, as is the recognition of the need for students to demonstrate measurable skills and capacities. For those reasons, we have identified these curricula as models of learner-centered design.

6

Assessment Aimed at
Learner Autonomy

Although many of us spend a tremendous amount of time thinking about and conducting assessments on our campuses, assessment is often still perceived as an onerous task, as evidenced by a recent article in the *Chronicle of Higher Education* titled "Assessment Projects from Hell" (Glenn, 2010). Hutchings (2010) writes that "unfortunately, much of what has been done in the name of assessment has failed to engage large numbers of faculty in significant ways" (p. 3). She acknowledges that the language of assessment has not always been welcoming, nor are faculty members trained in assessment. Likewise, work on assessment is rarely rewarded, and faculty members have not seen much evidence that assessment makes a difference. Yet assessment remains an essential component of what we do, and although not all assessments work the way we plan or give us the information we seek, effective assessment benefits everybody: institutions, administrators, faculty, and students.

Institutional benefits of assessment are many. Ongoing assessment at the institutional level gives administrators a picture of the health of the institution as a whole. Recall our analogy of the yearly physical exam—checking to see if any conditions have changed, particularly those of which we might not be readily aware. The results of those assessments should guide planning and decision making. Program faculty and administrators use assessment to monitor the success of academic plans to see if students are really achieving the established program outcomes. In a learner-centered model, these assessments are often embedded in the design of the curriculum to achieve specific purposes. Hutchings (2010) points out that "embedding assessment in the classroom sets the stage for work at the next level of the department or program, contexts which draw on what most members of the professoriate know and care most about: their discipline or field" (p. 13).

Assessment is also critical for teaching faculty. For faculty members, formative assessments can help them monitor whether learning is taking place throughout a course, and a combination of formative and summative assessments can help them determine whether course outcomes have been met.

Understanding Assessment in Learner-Centered Contexts

Students benefit from assessment too. Self-assessment helps us achieve two main objectives of a learner-centered curriculum: it helps students become more self-conscious or intentional about their learning, and it plays an integral role in the development of learner autonomy. In this chapter, we will address a variety of assessment practices and their application for these multiple audiences and purposes. Knowledge of and interest in assessment practices vary among faculty members and administrators. Our goal here is to demonstrate how specific assessment practices, many of which will be familiar to most readers, support a learner-centered approach. In other words, we're looking at some established practices through the lens of the learner-centered paradigm.

Monitoring Change

Assessment is about monitoring change, whether we are looking at classroom, course-level, or programmatic assessments. We define classroom assessments as the tools that teachers can use periodically throughout a course to monitor whether learning is taking place.

These assessments are formative by design. Course-level assessments, in contrast, are the mechanisms we use to determine whether or not students have met the stated learning outcomes for the class. Programmatic assessments are the mechanisms used to determine whether students have met the learning outcomes stated for the program. There is, of course, some overlap here, particularly if the design of the academic plan embeds assignments within specific courses to serve as programmatic assessments. The differentiation among these will serve as an organizing principle in this chapter.

Assessment does not lie solely with the teacher. Self-assessment and reflection are both important when we are talking about learner autonomy and making the learning process intentional for the student. Wasserman and Beyerlein (2007) make a distinction between these two forms of assessment. Self-assessment involves studying one's own performance in relation to strengths, improvements, and insights; reflection involves replaying a period of time to search for significance based on new learning. Reflection focuses on reconsidering what things mean and thinking about why one understood something a particular way at that time. Self-assessment, in contrast, focuses more sharply on evaluating one's performance. The assessment tools that we will present offer students the opportunity to do both.

Learning is about change, and although students will usually say that they are going to college in order to learn something or to get a degree in a specific discipline, they rarely say they are going to college to change themselves, which, in truth, is the goal. Sometimes it seems as if students think that they will follow the list of courses, put in their time, and obtain a degree, but that none of that will change them as individuals. But in truth, if the education process is successful, they will be different people when they emerge from the experience, and reflection will help them recognize that change.

Those of us who teach at institutions where students are the first in their families to attend college often see the difficulty students have as they begin to broaden their worldview and perhaps develop values and attitudes that differ from those of their family. That transition is a challenge but a necessary condition for learning. Recall Schön's definition of learning as the interactive process of assimilation. Providing ongoing assessment, particularly reflective assessments, can help students not only monitor but accept the changes they are experiencing. In Chapter Seven, we will reference two institutions that used electronic portfolios in this way and increased student retention as a result. When we as educators make assessment a focal point, learning becomes an intentional act for students.

Assessment also monitors programmatic change. Just as individual students can use assessment to monitor their growth and achievement of learning outcomes, faculty members and administrators can monitor program strengths and weaknesses through ongoing assessments. The authors of *College Learning for the New Global Century* make a good point when they write,

> Students should know from the time they enter college that they will be expected to complete milestone and culminating projects—"authentic performances"—to demonstrate both their progress in relation to essential outcomes and their ability to use the learning outcomes in the context of their chosen fields. (National Council for Liberal Education and America's Promise, 2007, p. 41)

The authors recommend that programs provide diagnostic, interim, and capstone experiences for students to see their progress on expected outcomes. Regular assessment of student learning, at the beginning, middle, and end—indeed throughout the academic plan—is a hallmark of learner-centered programs. Recall that we described the learner-centered curriculum as one that is built on a set of occurrences. We presented the Quest University curriculum as a model curriculum that hinged on several target points: the orientation, the formation of the student's question, the service component, and the capstone. In such a configuration, it would be only logical to embed assessments in these key elements of the curriculum.

A learner-centered academic plan must demonstrate that the program provides its graduates with demonstrable knowledge, skills, and abilities. More important, perhaps, is that students be able to identify what they have learned, where they have grown, and what they are able to do. Direct and indirect assessment can help us answer these questions with our students. Indirect assessments are those that are somewhat speculative in nature, usually in the form of surveys or reflections of reported perceptions about student mastery of learning outcomes. These perceptions may be self-reports by students or the perceptions of others, such as alumni, employers, or faculty. They are very useful forms of assessment, but must be accompanied by direct assessments. Direct assessments come in the form of tests, embedded assignments, and portfolios, with the emphasis on validity and reliability in measuring the achievement of learning outcomes. The combination of direct and indirect assessments provides multiple perspectives on the learning that is taking place, with the hope that the multiple measures support rather than refute each other. The use of multiple measures for assessment also is in keeping with our postmodern approach to curriculum design. Rather than allowing any single perspective to take precedence, we acknowledge the need for multiple perspectives that enhance and deepen our understanding.

Wiggins and McTighe (2005) explain that as we design programs, we should think as assessors, which means for them that we ask three important questions: (1) What evidence do we have that students have learned the stated outcomes? (2) What student assessments, tasks, or other evidence will support our academic plans and drive our instruction? and (3) What evidence will we use to understand the extent of our student learning? We will follow that guidance as we look at assessment options.

Establishing Student Learning Outcomes

The first step to any learner-centered assessment process establishes the student learning outcomes. Katz (2010, p. 5) points out,

> We know more than we used to about learning outcomes, but not enough. We know far too little, however, about how to put the knowledge we do have to practical use in transforming both our pedagogical technique and curriculum design to enhance student learning.

We will address these concerns in this section. In Chapter Three, we acknowledged that establishing learning outcomes, especially for some disciplines, can be a challenging task, but as we stated there, agreement on learning outcomes and how to assess them creates curricular coherence. When we set clear, demonstrable ways by which students will be asked to prove the achievement of the outcomes, then consistency among faculty members teaching a single course or across multiple sections of a single course increases. Thus, although achieving agreement on learning outcomes may be a challenge, the rewards of doing so are many.

Ideally, teachers have learning outcomes in mind for individual units within a course as well as for the course as a whole. Likewise, programs need stated learning outcomes. If we have used ideal learner-centered academic plan design, our academic plan is based on student learning outcomes. In other words, we began the process by asking, What knowledge, skills, and abilities do we want students to be able to demonstrate upon completion of our program and in individual courses? Our academic plan would then build on the established learning outcomes. As we mentioned previously, accrediting agencies can help with this stage of the process. In the health sciences, engineering and technology, and education, these outcomes are usually fairly explicit, with agencies either providing competency guides for the development of learning outcomes (as in the case of pharmacy which we will illustrate later), or specific learning outcome statements (as in the case of ABET's EC2000 standards). For business and liberal arts programs, accrediting bodies generally provide core topics (as in the case of the Association to Advance Collegiate Schools of Business [AACSB]); in the case of the Higher Learning Commission, for example, the directive is to have learning outcomes, but they are not specified.

Wiggins and McTighe (2005) discuss this initial planning phase. In the first stage, academic program designers determine appropriate results and outcomes. They ask, "What should students come away understanding, knowing, and able to do? What big ideas frame all these objectives?" (p. 147). For example, the Accreditation Council for Pharmacy Education (ACPE) standards for accreditation list professional competencies and outcome expectations. These statements are, according to the ACPE Web site, to "guide the development of stated student learning outcome expectations for the curriculum. To anticipate future professional competencies, outcome statements must incorporate the development of skills necessary to become self-directed lifelong learners." The first statement reads as follows:

> Provide patient care in cooperation with patients, prescribers, and other members of an inter-professional health care team based upon sound therapeutic principles and evidence-based data, taking into account relevant legal, ethical, social, cultural, economic, and professional issues, emerging technologies, and evolving biomedical, pharmaceutical, social/behavioral/administrative, and clinical sciences that may impact therapeutic outcomes.

Using this statement as a guide, the PharmD faculty at FSU developed twenty-one highly specific and measurable learning outcomes. In other words, the guiding statements provided by the accrediting agency aided the faculty in creating outcome statements.

When we developed the learning outcomes for the FSU BIS program, we did not have the benefit of an accrediting body to guide us other than the Higher Learning Commission, the accrediting body for the institution, which simply states that programs must have learning outcomes. We relied on some of the statements provided by the Association of State Colleges and Universities and the AAC&U regarding general education outcomes. From those we developed five general outcomes that we would expect of all graduates regardless of their chosen course or discipline preparation, emphasizing our viewpoint that a learner-centered curriculum is language intensive both in writing and speaking:

1. Graduates will demonstrate exceptional communication skills as demonstrated by written pieces in the program portfolio, including a personal philosophy statement, a skills assessment statement, as well as selected pieces of writing that demonstrate specific competencies of the individual's academic plan and general education.

2. Graduates will demonstrate exceptional presentation skills both in an oral presentation in the electronic portfolio that demonstrates the individual's specific competencies as outlined in his or her academic plan as well as the ability to articulate the interrelatedness of the separate disciplines within the academic plan.

3. Graduates will demonstrate self-assessment skills and the ongoing development of those skills in the program portfolio both in reflective journal assignments and semester assessment rubrics.

4. Graduates will demonstrate team-building skills as demonstrated through cooperative learning experiences in the orientation and capstone courses as well as individual service learning experiences.

5. Graduates will demonstrate discipline competencies including knowledge of content area as well as the ability to use the language of the specific disciplines demonstrated through selected works in the portfolio.

Then we ask students to develop, with our assistance, a minimum of three learning outcomes tied directly to their individual course plan.

According to Wiggins and McTighe (2005), in the second stage, planners determine what appropriate evidence exists of the desired results. Appropriate evidence might come from both formative and summative assessments, which are further discussed later in this chapter. In the case of our learning outcomes for the BIS, we embedded the evidence base in the learning outcome statement. It is important to note that before we can determine what evidence exists, we need to know what our goals or outcomes are. Huba and Freed (2000) write that "intended learning outcomes describe the kinds of things that students know or can do after instruction that they didn't know or couldn't do before. Formulating such outcomes may require a change of mindset" (p. 93). They note that for many of us, our course and program goals have focused on what *we* do, not on what our students will be able to do at the completion of our program or academic plan. Recall the *What if?* conversation on course descriptions in Chapter Four. If course descriptions were crafted around learning outcomes, students would be continually reminded that they need to demonstrate competencies. Huba and Freed continue that intended learning outcomes provide three major benefits: (1) they provide the foundation for assessment at all levels (course, program, and institution); (2) they inform instructional activity; and (3) they let students know what to expect from a course or program.

We accept Huba and Freed's premise that intended learning outcomes need to emphasize what students will be able to do upon completion of a course or program, not what teachers will do in the context of the course. For example, the first few of the twenty-one learning outcomes developed by the FSU pharmacy faculty associated with standard one of the ACPE guidelines read as follows:

> Level 1: Gather, organize and evaluate information in order to provide patient-specific and population-based disease management. Identify the concept, components, behaviors and values associated with patient-specific and population-based disease management (including determinants of illness, factors influencing the use of health services).
>
> a. Gather relevant information/collect data (via observation, interview, computer and other data bases) needed to provide patient-specific and population-based disease management.
> b. Describe the biological sciences (physiology, pathophysiology, biochemistry, microbiology, immunology, etc.) associated with the patient-specific and/or population-based disease management plan.
> c. Describe the pharmacology, medicinal chemistry, pharmaceutics, and pharmacokinetics of prescription, non-prescription and dietary supplements used in the patient-specific and/or population-based disease management plan.

Each of these actively phrased outcomes focuses on specifics of what students will be able to perform.

According to Wiggins and McTighe (2005), the third stage is to develop learning activities and teaching strategies to "promote understanding, knowledge, skill, student interest, and excellence" (p. 147). Course assessment measures should not be an afterthought in learner-centered academic plans; they should in fact drive the process and make the process of learning intentional for the student.

Applying Assessment in Learner-Centered Academic Plans

Individual Classroom Assessments

Individual class assessments—formative assessments used to monitor whether learning is taking place—might include such time-honored practices as asking students to list the most important or salient points from a period of classroom instruction as well as those points that continue to remain unclear or confusing. In this way, learner-centered teachers can assess both their success in providing students with opportunities for learning and those areas where more opportunities might be provided. Huba and Freed offer several examples for soliciting student feedback in courses, including what they call the muddiest point, the minute paper, the e-mail minute, the one-sentence summary, the word journal, direct paraphrasing, and application prompts (pp. 126–130). Before we talk about how these assessments work, we'd like to digress for a moment and explain *why* they work.

In 1977, Janet Emig wrote the paper "Writing as a Mode of Learning," which became the theoretical underpinning of the Write to Learn movement. Emig recognized that writing is unique in that it is integrative, connective, active, and available for visual review, thus making it the ideal form of assessment of learning. Writing is a learner-centered activity, in that it is constructive and requires the making of meaning on the part of the writer. Langer and Applebee (1987) presented evidence to show that activities involving writing foster increased learning and furthermore that different kinds of writing activities require thinking about content in different ways. Numerous studies on note taking, for example, revealed that note taking was a more efficient way of learning than listening or reading and that it was more productive than simply underlining. Later findings demonstrated that summary writing and note taking fostered comprehension but only superficial understanding, whereas essay writing promoted deep learning. Newell (1984) examined students' ability to recall information and apply concepts and reported that essay writing enabled students to "produce a consistently more abstract set of associations for key concepts than did note taking or answering questions" (p. 275).

The most effective assessments are going to involve writing because by reviewing students' writing, teachers are best able to gain insight into students' understanding of ideas and concepts. We know from our own experiences as students that we can think we know something (what Sviniki referred to as the illusion of comprehension), but when we go to put it into language, we quickly discover the holes in our understanding. And we see examples of this with student learning all the time. A colleague who teaches math found that asking students to write out their reasoning as they solved problems dramatically increased students' comprehension and success and allowed him to understand what the students' misunderstood. Writing to learn science has been widely successful in K–12 classrooms. Teachers have found that using a variety of modes, including critical essays, research projects, term papers, narrative journaling, situation-based fiction, and even dialogue, has greatly aided students not only in comprehending material but in understanding themselves in relation to that material. History teachers report that integrating writing throughout units increases students' grasp of content and the ability to learn how to think as historians. It is for these reasons that we believe that the most effective assessments are writing based. That's because meaning is in a continual state of emerging as we write, or as E. M. Forster is reputed to have quipped, "How can I know what I think until I see what I say?" The key here is that writing makes thinking visible. If the goal of assessment is to discover whether students are learning, the best way to see what is going on in their heads is to ask them to put that on paper. What follows are indirect measures of student learning that involve writing.

Formative Assessments

The kinds of ungraded writing assessments used for formative feedback focus on the content—that is, the student's understanding of the material. Because there is no grade attached and the writing doesn't even need to be returned to the student, teachers who do not feel comfortable grading writing assignments can still feel at ease using these techniques.

Muddiest Point, One-Minute Paper, and E-Mail Minute   The muddiest point, a precursor to the minute paper and the e-mail minute, was first introduced in Mosteller's article "The 'Muddiest Point in the Lecture' as a Feedback Device" (1989), which appeared in *On Teaching and Learning: The Journal of the Harvard-Danforth Center*. The basic premise is that in the last three to four minutes of a class section, the instructor asks students what the muddiest point was during the class period. This idea has been expanded to many areas, such as what is most unclear about a given task or assignment. The muddiest point has evolved into many student feedback systems, the best known of which might be Angelo and Cross's one-minute paper, described in their book *Classroom Assessment Techniques: A Handbook for College Teachers* (1993).

David R. Stead (2005) writes in his review of the one-minute paper that

> the OMP (alternatively known as the "minute paper" or "half-sheet response") is typically assigned at the end of a class, and requires each student to briefly write down answers to two questions, generally: (1) What was the most important thing you learned in class today? (2) What question is unanswered? As the name suggests, students are given a minute or two to complete the

exercise. After collecting the papers, the lecturer reads
the answers and ideally responds to them in the next
class, or privately on an individual basis. (p. 119)

As we stated earlier, the point of this assessment is for the teacher
to learn whether or not students are understanding key ideas. The
teacher can respond to the class as a whole about whatever requires
further explanation or revisiting, so no time has to be invested in
commenting on individual student responses or in handing back the
pieces of writing.

Teachers should carefully craft the prompts they use, taking
into account the depth of knowledge required for the response. For
example, asking students to summarize the key points of a lesson
requires different processing than asking students to explain the
relationship between today's lesson and a previous lesson or to
create a global statement about the point of the day's lesson. In
other words, as we choose assessment instruments, we need to be
intentional about what we want to find out. This goes back to our
discussion of the culture of assessment. We should ask questions to
which we really want to know the answers; we need to be genuinely
interested in what is happening.

The e-mail minute is a variation on the one-minute paper
that uses e-mail to elicit responses to salient points or question
prompts (Huba & Freed, 2000, p. 127). Huba and Freed describe
two methods for using the e-mail minute. The first is to collect responses to prompts and then for the instructor to read the responses,
identify common themes, and summarize them with comments in
an e-mail to the entire class. The other is to give the prompts
in class and ask students to respond via e-mail. Another variation
of this uses a discussion board post. We will discuss this a bit more
in Chapter Seven, which covers technology that can help us with
assessment and other features of learner-centered design.

Each of these approaches encourages students who might not
otherwise participate in class discussion. And as with all assessment,

as teachers we need to close the feedback loop—in other words, let students know that their input has been valued, taken into consideration, and responded to. Each of these methods should provide both student-to-teacher and teacher-to-student assessment opportunities, as students reveal their muddiest point and what they see as the most salient point and teachers summarize their observations for the class.

One-Sentence Summaries, Word Journals, and Paraphrasing   One-sentence summaries can be used for reading assignments or class sessions. These activities offer teachers insight into the level of processing going on. Can students summarize a specific topic or passage? This task requires students to process information and translate it into their own language. It can be used to have students summarize their understanding of the main or salient point from a lecture or discussion, enabling instructors both to measure student competency and to gain feedback on their own success. The one-sentence summary is a deceptively simple task. Students rarely realize that a limitation on the number of words or number of sentences increases the level of difficulty because it requires them to go beyond summary and regurgitation of notes and asks them to draw connections and articulate those "big questions" that Wiggins and McTighe refer to. One of our colleagues, for example, requires students to write a one-sentence summary of assigned reading in a drama class. Students can't simply repeat the plot but have to understand the theme and how it was executed in order to write the sentence. That calls for deeper understanding and the ability to make connections.

Word journals build on the same conceptual framework as one-sentence summaries and ask students to paraphrase part of a topic, class session, published work, and so on in a single word, and then to explain in a paragraph or two why they selected that particular word. A variation on this used by one of our colleagues gives students four terms to identify and then asks them to explain in one sentence what the four have in common. The trick to this is that when he constructs these exercises, he includes two terms that are pretty obviously related, one that is a stretch, and one that seems completely unrelated unless the students have a very deep understanding of each.

Direct paraphrasing expands on one-sentence summaries and word journals by having students paraphrase a topic, class session, published work, and so on for a given audience using their own words. This task assesses students' understanding and their ability to communicate to diverse audiences (Huba & Freed, 2000, p. 129). One approach takes difficult concepts and asks students to explain them to a ten-year-old. It is a challenging activity, not only relying on students' understanding the concept but also asking them to consider what contextual information would be necessary for the audience to understand in order to grasp the explanation.

Each of these methods could provide both student-to-teacher and teacher-to-student assessment opportunities, as teachers analyze summaries and paraphrases. It is unlikely that students would receive individual responses on such tasks, but teachers should close the feedback loop by reinforcing in their own summary or paraphrase what they see as the main point.

Application Prompts Application prompts build on the indirect assessment methods already described to have students consider how the new learning they have gained can be used or applied. These are ideal kinds of assessments, for they promote transfer and deep learning. In this method, instructors ask students to write down a real-world application for what they have learned. This activity helps measure both previous knowledge that is brought to the application as well as understanding of the present topic under consideration. It builds on students' abilities to summarize and paraphrase and calls for an application of learning. One of our colleagues in the College of Optometry has used this technique successfully for years. He teaches optics and asks students to maintain a journal in which they find everyday occurrences of the optical principles he has taught.

Huba and Freed provide an alternative approach to this method that asks students to think about possible applications for information that is about to be discussed in class. At the end of the class period, the instructor asks students to write down applications for one or two concepts. These authors note that such activities and methods reinforce the relevance of students' learning, and as we have stated, relevance is a key feature of learner-centered practices, as creating relevance improves motivation and also aids in establishing community.

These methods also provide both student-to-teacher and teacher-to-student assessment opportunities, as students apply course materials to these tasks. As with the other activities described, it is important to close the feedback loop and to share findings with students, as sharing with students is a visible example of Schön's interactive process of assimilation.

Each of the assessment examples in this section requires students to process information and put it into their own language, thus generating visible evidence of their understanding. One of the added benefits of these types of assignments is that students must take additional time to consider each element of course content. As Willingham (2009) explains from the viewpoint of cognitive psychology, "students remember what they think about" (p. 60). That seems like an obvious point, but he explains that there is a difference in memory processing that takes place when a person spends time thinking about a problem or issue rather than simply trying to remember or memorize that same information. Doing something with it, such as writing a line or two to the teacher, requires the student to think about it, thus aiding in memory retention. So the gains from these types of assignments are twofold, benefiting student learning and helping teachers monitor student learning. These assessments are not graded and thus require a minimal amount of time to review, but the results can be significant.

Summative Assessments

Unlike the ungraded formative assessments used by teachers throughout a course to determine if students are comprehending material, course assessments are normally graded, direct assessments tied to course outcomes. As important as indirect measures are to individual course and program quality, direct measures provide tangible evidence of learning—the proof. Direct measures are objective indicators of the achievement of specific learning outcomes. Such measures might include writing assignments, presentations, portfolios, artistic and creative work, extended research projects, tests, and, ideally, a combination of all these. The goal of direct assessment of student learning is to help both the instructor and the student to have a sense of the successes in the class and the areas that might need further attention. Direct measures of student success are generally evaluated by instructors, peers, or others.

In our opinion, all learner-centered curricula should be language intensive—in both written and spoken form—for the very reasons we discussed earlier in this chapter. Through the formation of language, individuals clarify their thinking; they must internalize the knowledge and form a deep understanding. Very simply put, if you cannot explain something either in writing or orally, then you do not know it.

Written Works   Writing assignments provide several opportunities for learner-centered teachers to make learning intentional for the student. First, writing assignments often require students to pull together information from disparate sources and disciplines to build their arguments. Writing allows for both depth and breadth in the exploration of an issue or issues of relevance to the course. Contemporary writing pedagogy encourages student-to-student interaction in peer review sessions and encourages recursive processes, including revision. In this way, students can grow in several areas through writing-based assessments: first, students produce a product that the instructor can use to assess students' understanding of content in the current course;

second, they produce a product that the instructor can use to assess students' overall abilities in interpreting, synthesizing, and applying information. Furthermore, collaboration in the form of peer review, which is typically a part of writing-based assessments, provides students with the opportunity to integrate information from multiple sources and to draw on their prior learning.

In "Application of Learner-Based Teaching Innovations to Enhance Education in Wildlife Conservation," Ryan and Campa (2000) state,

> Writing is a powerful pedagogical tool for developing critical thinking and retaining discipline-based information. The composition process can bring order and understanding to complex and confusing ideas. Writing to learn emphasizes the writer being engaged with problems or questions. It becomes the process of exploring ideas and creating a message rather than the passive reporting of the thoughts or conclusions of others. Writing to learn epitomizes active learning pedagogy.... By engaging students with the kinds of problems faced by wildlife professionals, the writing process itself becomes a powerful means of active learning in the discipline. Problems should stimulate curiosity or create intellectual dissonance that promotes the desire for new knowledge. (p. 175)

Writing provides opportunities for students to synthesize prior learning with current learning and to apply both prior and current learning to real-world situations. Ryan and Campa conclude,

> Drafting and redrafting a solution requires acquisition of knowledge and application of intuition and creative thought. Writing in a relevant context promotes discovery of linkages among existing ideas, the reshaping and reorganization of old ideas, and the creation of new ones. (p. 175)

Instructors can examine paper submissions to assess students' abilities to synthesize and apply the knowledge, skills, and abilities gained through their individual experience and through their academic plan. We recognize that not all teachers feel comfortable assessing student writing; the use of carefully crafted rubrics that focus on content rather than on expression or editing, however, can (1) alleviate a teacher's lack of confidence in grading writing, (2) make the task of grading far less time-consuming, and (3) make the results more objective and understandable for the students. Regardless of what students might like to think about the assessment of their writing, it is not a subjective process, particularly when instructors use rubrics that explain in precise detail the elements that they are evaluating. Over the past twenty-five years, rater training has increased the objectivity of writing assessment, even on a large scale, with the result that outcomes reliability is high.

A great example of this type of writing assessment was conducted by Carrithers and Bean (2008) in assessing critical thinking skills of finance majors. They embedded a writing assignment, in this case a memo, into a 400-level finance course as part of a take-home examination. Seven other finance faculty assessed the memos holistically, using a rubric that identified finance elements and six levels of response that incorporated increasingly more sophisticated levels of critical thinking. They concluded that their

> approach to assessing critical thinking based on a discourse rather than a psychometric theoretical model proved useful in identifying critical thinking problems exhibited by our students, suggesting possible ways to address these problems through changes in curriculum instruction, homework design, and promoting rich faculty talk about student learning. (p. 24)

Presentations Like writing assignments, presentations are an opportunity for interaction with and among peers. Presentations also require information to be pulled together, and they often allow for both depth and breadth of exploration of a given subject or subjects. Instructors can measure learning across courses and the students' ability to synthesize and integrate learning. Finally, students must hone oral presentation skills for such assignments; this is an area that many students are uncomfortable with but that our current world of work often requires.

In *Helping Students Learn in a Learner-Centered Environment*, Doyle states that telling students, "Your work will be made public!" can "significantly improve the quality and depth of students' learning experiences" (2008, p. 115); one of the main advantages of public presentations is increased accountability. Presentations can be used for each of the assessment types we advocate for in Chapter Three—teacher-to-student, student-to-teacher, peer-to-peer, and self. Certainly, students will be more accountable when they know their peers will hear their work. Students can be required to write a self-assessment of their presentation. The teacher will be a member of the audience, and he or she should provide feedback on the presentation.

Doyle (2008) cites two areas of performance assessment related to presentations: one is an evaluation of the quality of the presentation and how information is presented to the audience; the other is the quality of the information presented. Students must become much more familiar with information that they are about to present. Doyle also advocates for the use of authentic assessment in his examination of presentations. He writes, "Performance assessments provide an authentic measure of what students have learned. Authentic assessments expect students to complete a full array of tasks that mirror the priorities and challenges found in the best instructional activities" (pp. 115–116). And, as is the case with writing assessment, the use of rubrics greatly enhances the reliability of the rating and reduces any sense of arbitrariness in the assessment process.

Portfolios   Portfolios generally come in two types: the complete portfolio, which is a collection of every piece of work a student produces in a course; and the selective portfolio, which comprises the students' selection of their best writing, research, artistic, and creative works for evaluation and assessment. In the case of selective portfolios, students must critically assess their own work, and the instructor has an opportunity to see development and progression across the course. Portfolios are useful means of regularly assessing student learning at the beginning, middle, and end of a course, particularly if instructors have already given students feedback on the pieces used to construct the portfolio.

Portfolios offer several advantages as assessment tools. According to Huba and Freed, "One benefit is that the use of portfolios establishes faculty as the primary evaluators of our courses and programs" (2000, p. 259). That is, as subject-area experts, faculty are uniquely positioned and qualified to evaluate portfolios as part of course or program assessment. Portfolios also provide a wealth of information based on actual student work; they engage faculty in meaningful dialogues with each other and, particularly if part of a course, with students. For students, Huba and Freed argue that "when students participate in the selection, discussion, and evaluation of their work, they begin to develop a view of themselves as learners" (p. 262). In this way, portfolios become more than the compilation of student work. They require students to engage in metacognitive evaluations of their own work and allow them to examine their own individual growth and progress. Hutchings (2010) also emphasizes the importance of involving students in self-assessment, noting that while Alverno College remains the most noted pioneer in this effort, numerous others have joined in, including the Association of American Colleges and Universities (2002), in its push for intentional learning. Portfolios can be excellent sources of teacher-to-student assessment and student self-assessments. We will discuss portfolios further in the next chapter when we look at technology that supports assessment—in this case, electronic portfolios.

Artistic and Creative Work and Extended Research Projects   Artistic and creative work and extended research projects are opportunities for students to apply concepts across courses and disciplines to projects that challenge them to integrate their learning, and to develop creative capacities and demonstrate their knowledge, skill, and abilities. They are types of authentic assessment. Grant Wiggins, in an online interview at *edutopia* (www.edutopia.org/grant-wiggins-assessment), defines authentic assessment as follows:

> Authentic assessment, to me, is not meant to be the charged phrase, or jargony phrase that it has come to be for a lot of people. When we first started using it fifteen years ago, we merely meant to signify authentic work that big people actually do as opposed to fill-in-the-blanks, paper-and-pencil, multiple-choice, short-answer quiz, school-based assessment. So it's authentic in the sense [that] it's real. It's realistic. If you go into the work place, they don't give you a multiple-choice test to see if you're doing your job. They have some performance assessment, as they say in business.

Artistic, creative, and scholarly projects are useful because they replicate real-world activities, thus enhancing their sense of relevance for students. These kinds of projects, like public presentations, provide multiple means for assessment: peer-to-peer, student self-assessment, and teacher-to-student.

Well-structured, learner-centered courses will include multiple modes of assessment throughout the term of instruction. It should be clear to students from the outset of a course what they are learning and how they will be assessed, and students should understand that assessment activities will be used to evaluate both their individual performance and the success of the course.

Programmatic and Academic Plan Assessments

In the same way that we advocate using multiple direct and indirect measures of student learning in learner-centered courses, we believe that program assessment must be balanced, using a variety of direct and indirect measures that may already be in place at the institution. Programs might consider several of the same measures we discussed in the previous sections as either indirect or direct measures for program assessment.

Indirect measures include student satisfaction surveys or similar nationally normed or locally constructed instruments, exit interviews, graduate follow-up surveys or interviews, employer surveys, faculty surveys, focus groups, reflective writing and personal analysis, regular student-adviser and student-faculty meetings, and related activities.

Direct measures of student performance can include final capstone courses where presentations, portfolios, artistic and creative work, or extended research projects demonstrate student growth throughout their academic plan or program. One notable example was designed by Sum and Light (2010); they developed a one-credit course with a menu of innovative assignments and exercises aimed at measuring student ability in critical thinking, oral and written communication, and discipline knowledge in a political science program. The main activity is a simulated academic conference that serves as a direct measure of student learning outcomes.

> The primary benefit of the simulated academic conference is the direct assessment of artifacts for the department's key student learning goals. However, the activity has other, less tangible benefits as well. For example, the format introduces students to the academic profession. If instructors take the

role of chair and discussant seriously, the panels will generate deep discussion and new knowledge. Students can realistically and comfortably benchmark their knowledge and capabilities against those of their colleagues. (Sum & Light, 2010, p. 525)

The additional activities are also innovative and learner-centered. They require a mapping exercise that asks students to chart their instructional gains throughout the program, rating each course within the curriculum. There is also an open-ended exit survey and a "learning through teaching" activity that asks students to make team presentations in 100-level American government courses. The complement of assessments has proven to be very successful. According to Sum and Light, "The capstone generates many diverse and complementary results through its various activities and the use of multiple assessment mechanisms" (p. 526).

Direct measures of program success are generally evaluated by the program faculty. As discipline experts, faculty are well positioned to select assessment techniques that match their learning outcomes. Faculty should drive program assessment because of their expertise and their understanding of local contexts.

Further, faculty should drive program assessment because the information that is gained from assessment should be used to improve the program. Assessment provides program faculty with the information they need to revise the academic plan, revise learning outcomes, add or remove outcomes, and reimagine courses and learning opportunities. In short, assessment is the mechanism that program faculty should use to drive their program.

Indirect Measures of Program Success

Allen (2004) writes in *Assessing Academic Programs in Higher Education* that indirect measures work in concert with direct measures to

pursue issues in depth and to solicit advice from important stakeholders. For example, faculty might learn that
students are not mastering an important learning objective, but they may not know how to respond. They
could use an indirect technique, such as an interview
or focus groups, to explore this problem and develop an
informed response. (p. 103)

Surveys are a frequently used way of eliciting feedback. The
most common are employer satisfaction surveys, alumni surveys,
and student satisfaction surveys of their perceptions of learning.
Satisfaction or other surveys are a useful means of encouraging
students to critically examine what they have gained from a course
and from approaches taken to a course. Survey findings are indirect
measures, however, and results should be used with caution because
a person's level of contentedness is not a measure of his or her
learning. Survey results imply a relationship, but they best function
as an indicator of needed direct assessment.

FSU's Department of Languages and Literature used survey data
to trigger needed assessment of the upper-level writing courses.
Initially, we surveyed the students with regard to their level of
confidence performing specific tasks. We also surveyed the faculty
and asked them to rate, in general, the students' abilities in these
same areas. The results were diametrically opposed, indicating to
us that some direct assessment of those skill areas was called for.
The direct assessment results supported the faculty's assessment
of skills.

As AQIP reviewers, we have repeatedly found institutions
reporting graduation rates as indicators of student learning. This
erroneous use of data arises from a limited view of assessment
as a means of proving one's worth or quality rather than as an
expression of genuine curiosity about what students are learning.
Katz (2010) refers to this as a consumerist approach to assessment, driven in large part by the Spellings Commission on the

Future of Higher Education. He quotes the commission's repeated use of the used-car metaphor, claiming that Americans have more information about the used car they buy than the educational institution they choose and that it was time to "kick the tires" of our educational institutions. In other words, under pressure from outside agencies, in particular the federal government, educational institutions use assessment data to protect themselves and to sell their product rather than to assess student learning for continuous improvement.

We cannot emphasize enough the importance of genuine curiosity in planning assessment. It seems so simple as to go without saying, but before you can begin assessing something, you need to have a question in mind. What do you want to know? We have seen enough poorly designed assessment projects to believe that too often the process doesn't begin with that question.

Several nationally normed student perception and satisfaction surveys might provide useful data to programs interested in understanding what students are gaining from their programs; these include the National Survey of Student Engagement (NSSE), the Higher Education Research Institute's College Senior Survey, and the Indiana University Center for Postsecondary Research and Planning's College Student Experiences Questionnaire. These surveys largely focus on gathering student feedback on learning outcomes and campus environments. Each of these instruments, however, is focused on institutional assessment and may have limited applicability to programs if the institution as a whole does not participate in such surveys. Surveys of this sort can help faculty and administrators gauge some of those less easy to measure learner-centered qualities, such as community and power sharing, and are designed to capture environmental qualities that are indicative of a learner-centered program or institution.

Locally developed surveys can also yield many usable results. Such surveys use a variety of approaches to solicit student feedback, including open-ended questions to elicit students' thoughts on the program, and closed-ended questions that allow students to select from a menu of scaled responses (Allen, 2004). Allen warns that surveys should be carefully designed and narrowly focused to elicit responses that will be helpful to the program as a whole.

In previous chapters, we have emphasized the role of dialogue in the learner-centered curriculum and how learning takes place through continual dialogue. We can learn much through dialogue in the form of interviews or focus groups. Interviews, whether open-ended and conversational or focused on specific questions and answers, can provide faculty with important information on their program. Faculty can gain insight into student perceptions of their program and experience, growth and development, approaches to teaching and learning, and myriad additional areas. Allen writes that among the benefits of interviews is that they "provide a sense of immediacy and personal attention that often is lacking with surveys" (2004, p. 113). Interviews, then, can serve the dual function of both connecting students with programs and assessing programs. Interviews differ from surveys in that there is personal interaction in the interview, which Allen indicates is both a strength and a weakness of this approach, as interviewer bias can be introduced into the process.

Focus groups, like interviews, involve personal interaction. Allen writes that similarly to interviews, focus groups "provide personal interaction as data are collected and allow for probing questions and clarifications" (2004, p. 118). In focus groups, participants can hear one another's responses and build on them. Leading focus groups requires one to have an understanding of group behavior, to be able to multitask, and to manage the discussion. Allen recommends the use of impartial third parties to conduct such groups.

Reflective essays have the benefit of providing both direct and indirect feedback. Using focused questions, evaluators can assess progress on outcomes tied to writing and communicating while at the same time collecting data on student perceptions of the issues explored in the written prompt. Written responses may also provide more structured examinations of the issues a program is assessing. At the same time, students may not be as open and direct in their written work as they are in short, focused surveys and interviews.

Reflective writing, self-analysis, and self-evaluation or rating also provide opportunities for metacognitive growth and self-reflection. Self-analysis of growth can happen at any point in a program and may use any of the formats we have discussed. It asks students to reflect on their individual growth and learning in the program. Self-evaluation and rating are similar, but ratings often ask students to evaluate themselves using rubrics or Likert-style scales.

Progress logs are a type of reflective indirect assessment that we developed and use both in our individual classes and in our programmatic assessment of the BIS. In a course, students are given a three-column table: the first column lists the assignments; the second column requires students to list learning outcomes; the third asks students to list challenges. Each time an assignment is returned, students must identify which learning outcomes for the class were addressed in the assignment and then record errors and mistakes that they made—in other words, the challenges they have yet to overcome. Ideally, as the semester progresses, the learning outcomes for the course are all listed at some point in column two, and the list of challenges progressively decreases as the semester reaches closure. The table serves as a nice visual representation of students' learning and growth.

For programmatic assessment, we give students a form to fill out each semester asking which of the program outcomes they addressed that semester, which courses or activities addressed those outcomes, and how well they feel they have met the outcomes. We deliver the form to students electronically and, in order to maximize compliance with our ongoing assessment of the program, require them to complete it prior to having their registration hold lifted.

Direct Measures of Program Success

Direct measures of program success generally involve quantitative measurements. That is, the results are generally measureable with identified correct and incorrect responses or clearly identified standards of success, often measured through rubrics. Although good quantitative assessment can be conducted by faculty with no formal training in such approaches, Allen (2004) advises faculty to take advantage of the substantial resources available on many campuses and to be aware that a significant body of work exists on quantitative measurement.

As we discussed in the section on direct measures of student assessment, presentations, portfolios, artistic and creative work, and extended research projects allow students to demonstrate their learning and skill development in real-world application. The benefits of such direct measures are many, including positive interactions between peers and teachers and the opportunity to integrate learning from the multiple perspectives encountered in an academic plan. In program assessment, such measures should use norm-referenced evaluation, which might include the use of rubrics or norming sessions in their development. Ideally, several program faculty members as well as objective third-party observers are involved in evaluating these works as part of program assessment.

Although we do not feel that examinations are the best direct assessment of student learning in individual courses, there are many nationally normed examinations that might be of interest to programs, including the Area Concentration Achievement Test (ACAT), by PACAT; the Collegiate Assessment of Academic Proficiency (CAAP), by ACT; the Major Field Test (MFT); and the Proficiency Profile/Measure of Academic Proficiency and Progress (MAPP), by ETS. Both the CAAP and the MAPP primarily measure knowledge in general education areas, whereas the MFT and ACAT are both discipline-specific examinations.

Any of these examinations, in combination with other indirect and direct measures, can provide a benchmark for program assessment.

A balanced approach using both indirect and direct measures will provide the most complete assessment picture for the program. The FSU PharmD, for example, uses a robust automated assessment tracking program to monitor student progress on learning outcomes, down to the course level. They capture assessment data from multiple perspectives, including students, peers, teachers, and professionals when students work in clinical settings. The program currently relies heavily on indirect measures, primarily collected through survey instruments and interviews. As is the case in all professional pharmacy programs, however, students must complete the North American Pharmacist Licensure Examination administered by the National Association of Boards of Pharmacy. Pass rates on the examination serve as at least one direct measure of program success.

The importance of assessment in a learner-centered, integrated academic plan cannot be overstated. Assessment provides programs with the information they need to make curricular changes and to understand what and how students learn. Strong academic programs will participate in continuous improvement projects that allow them to constantly adapt to changes in students and in society.

Chapter Summary

In this chapter, we have presented a number of indirect and direct assessment options that teachers can use in individual classes to monitor student learning and also that can be worked into curriculum design in order to monitor student progress in a program. Most of the assessments that we discussed are not new, but we presented them in a slightly different context by showing how they help support learner-centered curricula. For example, we presented focus groups and interviews, two time-worn practices, as opportunities to have dialogue in order to learn about student perceptions of our programs, and made the point that there is much we can learn from these interactions. We emphasize the role of assessor as learner. In a learner-centered institution, everyone learns, and when we approach assessment, we should always do so with a genuine interest in learning about something, whether it is how effective one's teaching has been or how effective courses are within programs. Good learners always act on their new knowledge. When we do learn something about our students' learning, we need to act on it—or, in assessment jargon, close the feedback loop. Assessment helps us as faculty and administrators learn about our students' learning and keep the process of learning in the forefront of students' thinking—that is, make learning intentional.

7

Innovating Through Technology

In our opening chapter, we claimed that our proposed educational experiment differs from past failed attempts of the 1970s because of advances in research on learning that have taken place since that time, which serve as the basis for the learner-centered agenda. Here we would like to qualify that statement to some degree by recognizing the role that technology can play in supporting learner-centered goals. We encourage curricular changes that are supported by new research on learning and have the potential to be facilitated by advances in technology that support learner-centeredness.

In Chapter Three, when we discussed the need to design new curricula, we quoted O'Banion (1997), who identified the barriers to educational reform, specifically our inherited time-bound, place-bound, efficiency-bound, and role-bound educational structure. Overcoming these barriers is the primary challenge of creating a learner-centered curriculum, and in Chapter Five we presented some model curricula that have successfully overcome this traditional structure of education. They did so not only by employing learner-centered pedagogy but by making use of ever-improving technology to support that pedagogical shift. We cannot address the learner-centered curriculum without talking about technology and the many tools available that help us transform our teaching. As O'Banion (1997) wrote,

The learning college must be built on a firm foundation, a foundation of strong building blocks that can
support the many new programs and practices required
to operate a learning college. Those building blocks
are beginning to be put in place. New applications
of technology, new research on learning, progress with
assessment and outcome measures, and experimentation
with reengineering educational institutions to become
learning organizations are already being used by progressive institutions to create more learning-centered
environments. (p. 63)

O'Banion made that statement well over a decade ago, before
many of us owned cell phones, and the creator of Facebook was
still in junior high. Since that time, the Web has evolved from
a place where individuals could browse for information to a place
where individuals participate and create. West and West (2009)
describe this transformation: "Today the Web facilitates a new
age of participation that is close to Berners-Lee's original intent,
inviting users to participate, co-create, edit, and collaborate rather
than merely consume. We have moved from read-only to the read-
write Web" (p. 1). In this chapter, we will consider the changes
in technology that have taken place that can be used to support
learner-centered environments. We do so acknowledging that any
discussion of technology becomes rapidly outdated.

There are many new tools available to support and enhance
face-to-face learning environments as well as to build fully online
learning environments. We will limit our discussion to tools that
support face-to-face learning environments. We also acknowledge
that many fine texts already exist that discuss technology and pedagogy in depth. Our discussion will focus specifically on the learner-
centered curriculum rather than on individual courses, and we will
approach that discussion in terms of (1) circumventing traditional

barriers to experimental design—or, to use the metaphor we have previously employed, breaking down the walls—and (2) using technology to enhance the key features of learner-centered curricula, specifically learner autonomy, community, and assessment.

Emerging Trends

As we explore the rapidly changing higher education technology environment, we are mindful of Wilen-Daugenti's list of drivers of change in higher education presented in *.edu: Technology and Learning Environments in Higher Education* (2009), in which she writes that

> Institutions seeking to understand how the next generation of Internet technologies will make an impact on their students and schools need to be aware of current trends.

- College-aged students are rapid adopters of new technologies, devices, and applications.

- Web 2.0 and social networking technologies enable easier access to increasingly available education content and online expertise, offering a venue for contributing and sharing knowledge regardless of location.

- Students are taking more responsibility for their own learning.

- Credible content is continually available on the Web.

- Video has high-adoption rates and is a key medium in higher education.

- M-learning (mobile learning) is on the rise in higher education.

- Gaming will be a key medium used in higher education in the near future. (pp. 3–4)

These trends in student technology adoption are significant indicators. Although we recognize that many areas of the country do not have the accessibility that more urban areas provide and that the availability of technology tools varies widely from institution to institution, the presence of these technologies is still relevant as we consider how to create more learner-centered programming. It is also worth noting that the drivers cited by Wilen-Daugenti are not isolated to the traditional eighteen-year-old freshman. In fact, our experience has been that in the case of fully online learning, adult learners quickly adapt to the technology and outperform their eighteen-year-old counterparts touted as the digital natives. We believe that success with many of these tools has more to do with learner autonomy than with technical savvy. In learner-centered curricula, the goal is to develop learner autonomy. As learners become more adept at monitoring and taking responsibility for their own learning, their use of these tools will become more effective. For that reason, as we plan learner-centered curricula, we should consider the way technology is built into the curriculum in order to best capitalize on student readiness for independent learning. *The ECAR Study of Undergraduate Students and Information Technology, 2010* (Smith & Caruso, 2010), a study that cuts across age and demographic differences, reinforces that point. The authors conclude that the findings from the survey bring

> into sharp focus the degree to which students have become co-innovators with campus technologists in driving change in how learning is structured and delivered. Any effort to understand the changing university, and specifically how technology is undergirding

education change, will be incomplete and distorted, absent an understanding of the student technological world. (p. 26)

Breaking the Time-Bound Barrier

In discussing the time-bound nature of our education system, the National Education Commission on Time and Learning, a 1992 commission charged with studying the effect of a time-bound mentality, stated, "Learning in America is a prisoner of time. For the past 150 years, American public schools have held time constant and let learning vary.... Time is learning's warden" (quoted in O'Banion, 1997, p. 10). In Chapter Two, we looked at this view of time and learning through the lens of the instructional paradigm and determined that if we are to be learner-centered, we must become more flexible. A learner-centered approach calls for time as a unit of measure to be replaced with learning outcomes.

In Chapter Four, we addressed the challenge of breaking the time-bound barrier, noting that although we may not be able to completely break the rules, we can learn to bend by becoming more flexible in regard to student credit hours toward degrees, making transfer from program to program less of a penalty, and promoting ease of transfer from one institution to another. The FSU BIS program that we highlighted in Chapter Five is a good example of this flexibility toward credit hours. One of the features that is most attractive to students, particularly those who have studied at a number of institutions, is our willingness to accept credits from multiple subject areas. The challenge for students is to integrate all their learning and to recognize how disparate subjects inform one another. Although we must adhere to the requirement of 120 credit hours for a bachelor's degree, we do not require that those credits be limited to a single discipline.

Two of the model programs that we described in Chapter Five chose to break the traditional time configuration by adopting a block schedule. Although students still meet for the amount of time required for course credit in the rest of the realm, they study each course intensely within a four-week period, one content module at a time.

Technology can also serve to bend, if not break, the time-bound barrier. Supporting face-to-face instruction with online tools such as those offered through Blackboard and other online course management systems (CMSs) breaks down the constraint of 150 minutes of instruction per week. In addition to collaborative engagement and meaning-making activities, contemporary technologies can allow students to reflect on classroom activities and interactions as well as develop new interactions. Each of the model programs we presented in Chapter Five began with an orientation course. If we are to strategically build technology into our programs, then the orientation experience becomes an ideal setting to introduce these tools, not just in terms of the technical use, but more so for their desired effect.

One tool that helps us break the time-bound barrier is the lecture capture system (LCS). These systems, such as Tegrity, Mediasite, and Echo360, allow learner-centered faculty to capture their face-to-face classroom experiences and upload them to their CMSs or Web sites. In this way, students have the opportunity to review what took place in the class session and to repeat parts of the session that were unclear or confusing to them. The FSU PharmD, for instance, relies heavily on Tegrity. Students can relive the class lecture session repeatedly both from their personal computer and through a Facebook application on their cell phone. Although traditional lecturing is not the ideal learner-centered pedagogical strategy, the truth is that large lectures are not going away in the near future, and this technology offers some opportunity for recursion that was not heretofore possible. Later in this chapter, we will show how other tools transform our traditional conception of the lecture into a more learner-centered experience.

I (Roxanne) have used Tegrity when concurrently teaching sections of the same course fully online and face-to-face, uploading the face-to-face class discussion for the online section. The online students share a discussion board with the face-to-face group, where they continue the class discussion beyond the assigned class time. This strategy adds an odd sense of performance to the face-to-face discussions, as the students know they may be challenged later by online students regarding their positions.

We should also point out that such tools are not confined solely to lecture capture. They also offer students the capability of making oral presentations in an online environment. A colleague who is a professor of communication told us of the difficulty her department had in trying to provide online opportunities for public speaking. In her case, Tegrity has solved the problem, and students can now upload oral presentations to their professor's CMS.

Some critiques of such systems have focused on decreased classroom attendance or attention during class sessions, but we believe that such systems can do much to foster empowerment and autonomy in learners who use them to supplement their class time and to build on the learning, meaning making, and knowledge building that have already taken place. We would further question that if students meet learning outcomes, does it matter whether or not they caught the live version of the lecture?

Breaking the Place-Bound Barrier

Because today's students are rapid adopters of new technologies, they come to us with a facility for using technology—admittedly, for the most part, for social networking. However, their familiarity with mobiles, whether phones, iPads, or other "always connected" devices, makes experimentation with these devices for pedagogical purposes easier. Zero institutional cost associated with their use becomes an even greater bonus. For example, Twitter can be used as an in-class discussion tool, and Poll Anywhere can turn a mobile device into a personal response system, a tool we will discuss in greater depth when we look at technology and assessment. The possibilities are endless, and for that reason, mobile technologies top the list of emergent technologies that will have an impact on teaching and learning.

The use of online discussion boards and chat rooms breaks down the barrier of time as well as place. Two easy ways to maintain an ongoing discussion of a topic are discussion boards and wikis. In the FSU BIS, for example, all students in the program are in a course shell called BIS Advising. This course shell offers the opportunity to communicate with students in the program throughout the semester, send reminders about registration, and have an ongoing discussion of integrated learning to which students must post at least once per semester.

In a dramatic example of breaking down the walls through technology, the Museum of Science in Boston collaborated with Tufts University to create a mobile application called Firefly Watch, which permits local residents to aid university scientists in a study of regional firefly populations (Johnson, Smith, Willis, Levine, & Haywood, 2011). Although this is not for course credit, it is certainly representative of the possibilities that technology affords.

Recently, wikis have grown in popularity as teaching tools. Like a threaded discussion, the wiki is an asynchronous communication tool; but unlike the threaded discussion, it is dynamic in that participants add, change, and even delete others' writing. For that reason, wiki access can often be restricted to registered users for posting and making changes, but can be distributed in such a way that it is open to the public for access to the information presented. This feature can be used to create a sense of authenticity for students' work and to provide a platform for truly public performance! The other feature of a wiki that is in keeping with our conception of learner-centered design is its nonlinear and multipage construction. These environments allow for deep collaborative learning while minimizing the risks associated with fully public databases. They also break down the place-bound barrier by opening the wall of the classroom to outside interaction.

In Chapter Three, we defined rigor as integrative learning that is self-organizing by nature. The blended learning environments we advocate encourage rigor in several ways. First, they encourage student interactions beyond the four walls of our typical classroom spaces. Through e-mail, synchronous chat, or asynchronous discussion boards, technology encourages interaction and integration. Our experience suggests that discussion board posts are more likely to include information from other courses and reading because they encourage reflection, integration, and synthesis. In short, Internet technologies promote rigor in learner-centered environments.

Weigel (2002) elaborates on this point when he writes that

> depth education is a hybrid or blended approach to e-learning that combines the best features of the brick-and-mortar classroom with virtual environments. In contrast to approaches that use e-learning technologies as another delivery system for traditional education, depth education can be implemented in a holistic fashion across the disciplinary span of college and university curricula, thereby placing e-learning at the core of the curriculum. (p. 23)

The approach that we advocate is one in which face-to-face education is enhanced through the strategic use of technology. We do not believe that we are headed for total online education for everyone, and the results of the ECAR *Study of Undergraduate Students and Information Technology, 2010* (Smith & Caruso, 2010), which we referenced earlier in this chapter, support that belief. For the past six years, students have consistently responded that they want only moderate use of technology in courses. "Whatever the underlying reasons, ECAR student survey respondents' views of IT in courses suggest that they still want face-to-face interactions in the classroom and with faculty" (Smith & Caruso, 2010, p. 93). So although we can use technology to experiment and to create richer learning environments, we need to choose our tools carefully and with moderation in order to achieve the fullest effect.

Fostering Autonomy Through Technology

At the beginning of this chapter, we referred to the drivers of change in higher education, among them students taking more responsibility for their own learning. We would like to believe that this is true, although those of us interacting with freshmen on a regular basis will approach that statement with considerable cynicism. Part of the learner-centered agenda creates opportunities to foster learner autonomy so that students learn to take responsibility for their own learning, and technology can certainly assist in that effort. McConnell (2006) writes that e-learning promotes what he calls "just-in-time learning":

> There are at least two processes underpinning the development of just-in-time knowledge. The first is "communication" where the focus is on exchanges and collaborative learning. The objective is to foster knowledge-building through social interaction. . . . The second process is "knowledge-building," and the focus here is on collective knowledge-building from exchanges between students and tutors, and students and students. (p. 16)

McConnell's knowledge-building process builds on empowerment and autonomy. Current electronic learning technologies promote autonomous student learning when they require students to develop knowledge themselves through both collaborative engagement and individual reflection. Miller (2009), a cognitive psychologist, makes even greater claims for online tools:

> From a memory standpoint, not only are online teaching tools acceptable, they're in many ways superior to more traditional modes of instruction. Although the study of memory is still at a relatively early stage, cognitive researchers have managed to nail down a number of principles that govern why we remember—and forget—what we do. Instructional technology meshes remarkably well with several of these principles, opening up new ways for us to make course material memorable. (p. 16)

In addition to enabling collaborative engagement and meaning-making activities, contemporary technologies are writing intensive, which we have argued is an essential characteristic of learner-centered curricula. We would add that although writing instruction itself has benefited from technology, all disciplines employing online tools, whether e-mail, chat, discussion boards, or wikis, become more writing intensive as a result of the tools themselves. Often, students have inadvertently learned important lessons about the power of language and about miscommunication through their use of these tools.

Building Community Through Technology

One of the major features of technology in learner-centered curriculum design resides in its ability to build communities. As the Web continues to evolve as a digital commons, the opportunities for students to form communities vastly increase, and students become more aware of the multiple communities or social networks to which they belong. As West and West (2009) note,

> Online educators now have an expanded tool set to support student-centered instruction and collaborative learning. Online students are no longer restricted to

> passive browsing, page reading, message posting and
> other individual learning activities. In the digital
> commons, online students have the capacity to become
> collaborative partners in the knowledge-building
> process. (p. 1)

As mentioned earlier, several technologies exist today that promote the creation of community, including such virtual learning environments as CMSs provided by Blackboard or open source developers, discussion boards, wikis, and multiuser virtual environments. The community-building benefits of technology should be clear to us today with the growth of online social media platforms such as Facebook. Our students are already connected to each other and to others in more formats than was previously imaginable, and we can harness these relationships for the benefit of student learning. Many academic programs have already developed a Facebook presence used to network among students as well as future students and alumni, and the increasing popularity of mobiles provides, in the words of the 2011 edition of *The Horizon Report*, a doorway "to the content and social tapestries of the network, and they open with just a touch" (Johnson et al., 2011, p. 12).

CMSs can be used to extend collaboration on projects beyond the classroom. Many systems today can be used to organize peer review and conference sessions in both synchronous (students logged in and working at the same time) and asynchronous (students using the system as their time allows) environments. In *E-Learning Groups and Communities*, McConnell (2006) writes,

> Networked collaborative e-learning is based on princi-
> ples of action learning and action research. The focus of
> study is largely problem-centred. Students should have
> as much choice as possible over the direction and con-
> tent of their learning. They arrive at the focus of their

studies through discussion and negotiation with other students and teachers.

It is based on critical reflective learning in a social context. The technology of networked collaborative e-learning supports group and community discussion and the sharing of experience. A social, conversational context is important in the process of learning since it supports the clarification of ideas and concepts through discussion. (p. 15)

This technology can use curriculum design to focus on key points within the curriculum either for assessment or for the curricular coherence we referred to in Chapter Six.

Game design has been identified as one of the emerging technologies on the horizon as a tool for enhancing learning. Alexander (2008) notes in "Games for Higher Education: 2008" that games can promote constructivist pedagogy if players reflect on their learning, perhaps through the use of blog posts, discussion threads, wiki comments, or podcasts; and if learners create computer games, they learn both gaming and content.

The Horizon Report (Johnson et al., 2011) defines game-based learning broadly to include social game environments; goal-oriented, nondigital games; commercial games for developing team and group skills; and role-playing games and simulations.

Gaming is an expansive category, ranging from simple paper-and-pencil games such as word searches all the way up to complex, massively multiplayer online (MMO) and role-playing games. Educational games can be broadly grouped into three categories: games that are not digital; games that are digital, but that are not collaborative; and collaborative digital games. (p. 20)

Of interest here would be the third category, collaborative digital games. Collaborative games have unlimited potential. Johnson et al. (2011) claim,

> Games like these, which occur in both massively multiplayer online (MMO) and nondigital forms, can draw on skills for research, writing, collaboration, problem-solving, public speaking, leadership, digital literacy, and media-making. When embedded in the curriculum, they offer a path into the material that allows the student to learn how to learn along with mastering, and truly owning, the subject matter. (p. 22)

Although the potential for gaming and games technology is vast, it is a field still in its relative infancy in higher education. Particularly on the scale of an entire learning plan, gaming platforms are only just beginning to enter higher education. However, their influence on the current generation of students and on future generations cannot be overstated. The ways in which students perceive the world, interact with one another, and solve problems have all been influenced by their exposure to computer games and gaming. That is not to say that experimentation is not taking place in higher education. The University of Wisconsin-Madison, for example, uses an engineering game called Cool It that teaches students about cryogenics. It also uses a game-based learning tool to teach students how to read and compose music. Similarly, the Boston College School of Nursing has created a virtual forensics lab for teaching crime-scene forensics (Johnson et al., 2011).

The significance of gaming is twofold: first, in terms of helping students achieve skills in our information-based culture; and second, in the way that gaming content can overlap with discipline content, providing an innovative way for students to engage with content (Johnson et al., 2011). "As this area continues to expand, and as game designers continue to explore new ways to integrate serious topics and content area in engaging formats, gaming will become more useful and more prevalent in higher education" (p. 26). Games also have strong potential for promoting integrative learning as gamers are required to apply knowledge from multiple areas to solve the problems presented by the game.

Using Technology to Assess

In the previous chapter, we discussed the role of assessment at both the course and programmatic levels. We cautioned that we need to be strategic in our assessment plans and instruments. In this section, we will cover a variety of tools that are available for gathering data. The fact that a tool can make assessment data more easily retrievable does not necessarily mean that the tool is effective in a learner-centered way. This is particularly true in the case of student response systems and online tests and quizzes. These tools need to be used with an understanding of learner-centered principles in order to achieve the desired outcomes, and the necessity of learning how to use these tools in a learner-centered way is mentioned by researchers in both cases.

Classroom Communication Systems

At the course level, classroom communication systems (CCSs), also called student response systems, personal response systems, or, more commonly, clickers, provide teachers with immediate feedback on student learning. These systems are not really emerging technology, as they have been used since the 1960s; however, as is the case for all technologies, advancements have been made over time. Judson and Sawada (2002) report that in studies spanning four decades, students have consistently supported the use of these systems, reporting that they enjoyed better comprehension as a result.

> Polls from the 1960s through the late 1990s found that
> the use of electronic response systems made students

more likely to attend class, pressed them to think more, prompted them to listen more intently, and made them feel instructors knew more about them as students. (p. 177)

When student achievement was correlated with the use of CCSs, however, there was no indication that use of the systems improved student learning except when they were used in a constructivist approach. This is a key point that is repeated by later research. The use of CCSs provides lecturers the opportunity to transform the large lecture hall, the icon of the instructional paradigm, into a truly learner-centered, engaging environment. We emphasize the word "opportunity." Judson and Sawada conclude,

One cannot assume that the existence of this type of technology will actually facilitate constructivist teaching, let alone academic achievement among students. Nevertheless, to provide the best opportunity for success, this review of literature suggests that institutions invest as much if not more in the pedagogical development of faculty as they do in the technology. (2002, p. 179)

A report by the University of Massachusetts Physics Education Research Group (Beatty, 2004) identified both the challenges to teachers and the resulting benefits of CCSs. Their findings are the result of more than ten years of experimentation with the technology. Their experience has led them to conclude,

By engaging their minds in class, CCS-based instruction makes students active participants in the learning process. This engagement results in more learning than the traditional lecture format offers and in learning of a different kind: students develop a more solid, integrated,

useful understanding of concepts and their interrelation-
ships and applicability. (p. 6)

As noted by Judson and Sawada (2002), however, the biggest
drawback is the retooling of instructor roles. Along with learning
the technical skills of authoring, editing, and arranging questions
in the system, the instructor must

> plan curriculum around questions and deep compre-
> hension, rather than around lecture notes and content
> coverage. The art of designing effective questions is
> deceptively nontrivial and can be time-consuming for
> an instructor new to CCSs. (With experience, the
> process can become as efficient as traditional lecture
> planning.) (p. 6)

What they describe is the transformation that is needed to be
learner-centered. Beatty goes on to say,

> the most daunting aspect for many instructors may
> be the necessity of giving up control of the class. A
> lecture is predictable and controlled, with attention
> safely focused on the instructor. CCS-based teaching,
> on the other hand, necessarily turns the classroom over
> to students while they debate in small groups and while
> they discuss their reasoning after the histogram display.
> (2004, p. 6)

The use of CCSs does not ensure that a transformation to learner-
centered pedagogy will occur. The CCS is simply a tool, one that
can be used badly, but as with the other technology tools we have
introduced, it provides an opportunity for those whose goal is to
create a learner-centered environment even in a large lecture hall.

Course Management Systems

Likewise, CMSs allow teachers to interact with students to assess responses, e-mail summaries to students, and maintain student portfolios. Tools are also available that allow teachers to construct multiple short responses in CMSs that ask students to provide feedback on specific learning activities, assignments, or topics. Surveys can be constructed on SurveyMonkey or similar survey tools to measure students' individual learning styles. We should note here that SurveyMonkey is available in a limited version (ten questions, one hundred responses) free of charge, but larger-scale survey options are available at a charge, depending on the size of the survey. Later in this chapter, we will describe how the FSU PharmD uses its CMS to create a type of electronic portfolio for assessment purposes.

CMSs feature the ability to administer quizzes and examinations in a variety of configurations. A study sponsored by the Pew Charitable Trust and conducted by the Center for Academic Transformation at Rensselaer Polytechnic Institute invited twenty institutions to engage in course redesign using technology, with the goal of improving student learning outcomes while reducing costs. Each participating institution focused on different technologies and different purposes. Six of the participants incorporated online assessment into their redesign. They found that the low-stakes quizzes motivated students and encouraged time on task. They reported that "online quizzing encouraged a 'do it till you get it right' approach: students were allowed to take quizzes until they mastered the material" (Twigg, 2003, p. 2).

This finding was confirmed in a recent study by Bunce, VandenPlas, and Havanki (2006), which found that quizzes and examinations administered through CMSs were more effective than the use of student response systems, a finding they attribute to the reflection time allowed by the CMS quiz, in contrast to the rapid responses of CCSs. Similarly, Marcell (2005) studied the effectiveness of online quizzing in psychology, and determined that quizzing regularly in an online environment assisted students in developing a regular reading and study schedule, with the end result being improved learning outcomes in the course.

Technology can also help assess at the programmatic level. For indirect measures, various options are available that can improve response rates on satisfaction surveys and exit interviews. Creating satisfaction and feedback instruments has become much easier with tools built into CMSs; online sources, such as SurveyMonkey; and commercial instruments, such as the IDEA Center's Student Rating of Instruction (SRI). The SRI can be administered electronically, with regular e-mail reminders from the IDEA Center to those who have not yet responded.

Collecting data on direct measures has also become easier to manage thanks to technology. Banta, Jones, and Black (2009) compiled profiles of good assessment practices. They noted that "technology can become a useful tool for organizing, implementing and sustaining assessment" (p. 129). Of the institutions they profiled, some have chosen to outsource data collection and management to external companies, whereas others have designed their own internal systems. Regardless, the technology was the key to sustaining assessment. The FSU PharmD program, for example, investigated several electronic portfolio systems but in the end determined that the campus CMS would meet its immediate needs, as there are products on the horizon designed especially for health care programs and specifically for pharmacy. The system that the FSU PharmD has adopted is simple, cost-effective, and, for the time being, gets the job done.

Students are now asked each semester to write a reflective piece on their progress toward becoming a professional, thus providing feedback on different aspects of professional development. In the first semester, the journal entries relate to entry into the PharmD program and self-perceptions as a professional; in the second semester, students reflect on development of a poster assignment completed in the Drug Delivery course. They post their piece to the discussion board designated for that assessment using a journal-format discussion topic so that other students cannot see their entries, but faculty can. A grading form is attached so that the assessment team can quickly read and assess each journal entry; the data are collected in the grade book. These data are then entered into TracDat, the campuswide relational database for tracking assessment outcomes, as a means of monitoring students' increased sense of professionalism.

Students are also asked each semester to respond to a survey to assess the ability-based outcomes for their respective professional year. They evaluate the content delivery in the first year of the program in regard to content duplication, integration, and omission from the approved syllabus. This is also conducted in the CMS as well, using the survey function of the assessment tool. The ability-based outcomes have been built into the survey tool, and students simply rate the degree to which the outcome was met. The results are easily collected and again entered into TracDat.

Electronic Portfolios

Electronic portfolios are becoming increasingly popular tools both for ongoing student reflection and for assessment. Barrett (2004) identifies three sometimes conflicting uses of electronic portfolios: (1) documenting attainment of standards, (2) collecting digital stories of deep learning, and (3) serving as marketing and employment tools for students upon graduation. She cautions that decision makers need to consider their purposes, because depending on the type of portfolio, different types of technology are required:

> A learning portfolio can be supported very nicely with a web log environment ("blogs"), whereas an assessment portfolio that ties artifacts to a set of standards, with feedback or validation, is best implemented

through a relational database structure. A marketing or employment portfolio only needs an authoring environment that supports formatting and hyperlinking on a web-based server. (p. 2)

Barrett (2004) further examines the differing perceptions about portfolios and their use. Some institutions use portfolios as summative assessment tools; others see the portfolio as a narrative learning tool. Barrett recommends a three-part portfolio system that includes an archive of student work, an assessment management system to document achievement of standards, and an authoring environment where students can construct and reflect. We do not necessarily favor one use over another, but we do think it is important to recognize the different purposes and uses of portfolios as we make decisions about our assessment plan.

LaGuardia Community College, which was part of the AAC&U Integrated Learning Project, reported that the e-portfolio (a learning portfolio model) helped students overcome fragmentation and make connections that supported their academic growth and success. In LaGuardia's project, students began compiling the portfolio the very first semester. The project leaders found that the e-portfolio helped students connect classroom, career, and personal goals and experiences; the e-portfolio moved students toward not only integrated learning but also more integrated lives. Portland State University, also a participant in the AAC&U Integrated Learning Project, reported similar success with e-portfolios of this type. These two examples illustrate the distinction that Barrett makes between assessment *of* learning versus assessment *for* learning: "Assessment for learning provides firm evidence that formative assessment is an essential component of classroom work and that its development can raise standards of achievement more effectively than any other strategy" (2004, p. 4). As we noted in the previous chapter, programmatic assessment requires both formative and summative assessments.

Many options are available for electronic portfolios, and it is easy to be seduced by the robust attributes that some packages promise. These packages are usually mechanisms for collecting widespread institutional data for summative assessments and for creating marketing portfolios for students to use upon graduation. Barrett (2004) refers to these commercial packages as "deanware," as they are meant to appeal to administrative needs for data collection. It is also important to remember that in the end, human beings still have to do the assessing. So as attractive as it may seem to have a systemwide portfolio that papers can be submitted to for archiving, by necessity, someone is going to have to read those papers. Our caution is simply this: be strategic. The purpose of gathering data is to use them, and more is not always better.

In the previous chapter on assessment, we recommended that learner-centered curricula plan, within the design of the program, for regular assessments of student progress toward programmatic learning outcomes. It is at this point in the design process that assessment questions need to be asked and answered. Embedded assessments are excellent choices because they increase the motivation for the student and they reduce workload in the sense that they do double duty. A few well-conceived embedded assessments, perhaps delivered in a CMS, can produce valuable feedback regarding the effectiveness of the program and the student learning that is occurring while also providing convenient and accessible storage of assessment data.

In our chapter on assessment, we emphasized oral as well as written presentations. With the technology available today, oral presentations can be easily incorporated into electronic portfolios for programmatic assessment. The same is true for many capstone projects, for artistic and creative work, and for extended research projects.

Chapter Summary

The growing importance of technology in teaching and learning can hardly be overstated. As computing technologies have become more ubiquitous in everyday life, they have also become central to university education outside the disciplines that originally spawned them. In this chapter, we have shown how technology can be used to break down some of the barriers to creating truly learner-centered curricula. The various technologies presented foster learner autonomy, community building, and deep learning; and, with the advent of new gaming technology, experiential learning can also be added to this list. In addition to helping teachers monitor ongoing learning in their courses, technology can also support our efforts to assess student learning in our curricula. Thus technology tools can facilitate best practices in teaching and learning.

8

Learning Spaces That Support
Learner-Centered Curricula

We began the Preface with an analogy between curriculum design and classroom design in order to make the point that pedagogical innovations within individual courses oftentimes cannot reach maximal effect if confined to a structure that is not conducive to flexibility and innovation. Remember that lovely new furniture placed in rooms so small that the pieces couldn't be moved around as they were designed to be used? We have also made reference in several places throughout the book to the role that physical space can play in curriculum revision. In the case of the FSU PharmD, we noted that physical constraints prevented the program faculty from making all the curricular changes they wanted to make; we also suggested that tying curriculum design to classroom renovation was a logical and positive incentive to offer to curriculum innovators. In this final chapter, we explore the implications of all these references.

Building projects are rewarding because there is something tangible to see at the end of the day, which is not the case for most of the work we do. Likewise, building or renovation projects can create energy and enthusiasm on a campus, so it only makes sense to capitalize on that energy and enthusiasm to help us reach compatible goals. We will consider the role that physical space plays in learning and subsequently how renovation of spaces can be used to promote curriculum revision. However, many places don't have money for new buildings right now, so we will also consider some low-cost options that can have an impact on curriculum.

We will begin by looking at some general issues related to physical spaces and learning, first examining physical spaces in the instructional paradigm followed by a consideration of research on the impact of physical space on learning. We will then look at some of the innovations in classroom design that have been implemented at colleges and universities.

Physical Spaces as Learning Environments

When we have referred to learning environments previously, we have been referencing pedagogical strategies that create community and foster active learning. In this chapter, we think about the physical learning environment—classroom, study, and gathering spaces specifically—and how physical spaces can support those pedagogical strategies. We want to remember that space can be an agent of change, and as we will discuss later in this chapter, physical changes can carry symbolic impact and foster, as well as support, pedagogical change. Similarly, physical spaces can provide visible, tangible reminders of our intentional shift toward a new paradigm.

Though we are probably aware of it on an unconscious level, more often than not we ignore the impact that physical spaces can have on learning. Department chairs are usually the first ones to hear about such obvious issues of comfort as heat, light, and noise, and they are typically the ones who deal with complaints about rooms not conducive to the instructor's teaching style or subject matter, but they are often limited in their ability to respond to faculty who bring these issues to them. So, many of us continue to find ourselves teaching in spaces from another era that present us with various challenges. Because we are not afforded the opportunity to renovate rooms on a regular basis or build new facilities, most faculty tend to make due. However, by being aware of the importance and effect of physical space on learning, and by remaining sensitive to the impact of room arrangement and aesthetics, we can make adjustments and modifications where possible and seek creative solutions to the challenges these spaces present.

When designing our courses and considering effective practices for our classes, we should also take time to consider the physical classroom environment. There are institutional behaviors that sometimes hinder our best efforts—for instance, when the custodial staff dictate seating arrangements. Nonetheless, we need to make the necessity of appropriate learning spaces a main concern that is addressed institutionally, one that becomes part of planning and is recognized as a priority at all levels of administration.

Rethinking Our Use of Space

Thomas Fisher, dean of the College of Design at the University of Minnesota–Twin Cities, was quoted as follows in a roundtable discussion of campus sustainability:

> I think campuses are headed not so much to a cliff but toward a brick wall. Tuition has risen far faster than inflation. . . . We are going to be less affluent in this country, and our institutions are going to be less affluent. And what I hope comes from that is not just trying to maintain the old paradigm and watch everything slowly decay, but that we actually go through the paradigm shift and fundamentally operate in a different way—a sort of rediscovering of what we are. (2007, p. 38)

Interesting that he refers to a paradigm shift. Our focus thus far has been on reconfiguring curriculum to reflect the values of the new paradigm. Shifting paradigms seems to be a bit like painting and carpeting a room in your house. Once you finish one room, you realize how shabby the other rooms look, so the renovation must continue. In shifting to a learner-centered paradigm, the original focus was on pedagogy within individual classrooms. Once those changes began, we could see the need for changing the design of the curriculum to fit the new way of teaching, and now we would like to consider the spaces that house that curriculum and what changes are needed to support it.

Beyond issues of comfort, a variety of other factors play a role in the physical nature of the learning environment. On a very basic level, the arrangement of furniture in a classroom can affect the flow of communication and send messages to individuals about power and control as well as about our expectations of learners. Later in this chapter, we will show how the colors and aesthetics of a room also have the power to reinforce learning and encourage participation.

In the previous chapter, we referred to O'Banion's contention that schools are place-bound and that this makes change very difficult. He quotes George Leonard from a 1992 article in the *Atlantic*, "The End of School," that likens the traditional classroom to an isolation cell, a jail. He goes on to comment, "If the student is to be freed for more powerful learning experiences and if the teacher is to be freed to facilitate that learning in a more powerful way, then the walls must crumble, the boundaries made limitless" (1997, p. 11). He continues,

> If reform efforts are successful, the campus, the class-room, and the library will be turned inside out. A few structural elements will remain to serve the needs of those students who learn well in a place-bound context. But for the most part, these place-bound constructs will be artifacts, abandoned by the majority of students and faculty who will learn to use the open architecture created by new applications of technology and by new knowledge about how human being[s] learn. (p. 12)

This is not to say that the brick-and-mortar university will become obsolete as we continue to move into an online educational environment, but the brick and mortar will feature new open designs that support learning, collaboration, creativity, and so on. The Society for College and University Planning (SCUP) has published two volumes titled *Educational Environments* that feature the outstanding achievements in new facilities across the United States. In the preface to the second volume (Yee, 2005), Carole Wharton, president of SCUP, writes,

> At first glance the projects in this volume may appear to be about the physical environment, but upon closer examination, you will sense the potential that they have unleashed for learning at many levels—physical, emotional, cultural, intellectual—and for creating an enduring sense of place.

We will present some of these open designs throughout this chapter as examples of physical spaces that support learner-centered pedagogy.

In addition, we will argue that as we modify our traditional campuses in order to be responsive to the changing environment of higher education, we must keep in mind what we know about environments that foster creativity. Spaces need to support collaboration, teamwork, and community if we want to develop creativity. And although the longitudinal data from the Cooperative Institute Research Program (Higher Education Research Institute, 2011) indicate that the student profile hasn't really changed much over the past fifteen years, it is true that students do have expectations based on their experiences, and, as we pointed out in the previous chapter, technology plays a big part in their lives, so those open, collaborative spaces also need to support technology.

Those of us who have taught for more than a decade or two are constantly reminded of the differences in new generations of students. A colleague related a story that illustrated one facet of these differences. She had made arrangements with a student to attend one of her classes in session in order to make up a test. When the student arrived, the class was engaged in peer-group discussions. Our colleague began trying to think of an alternative way for the student to make up the test because she assumed that the noise would be a problem. The student simply pointed to his ear buds, which would block out any classroom distraction, and indicated that the noise wouldn't have bothered him anyway. Quiet is no longer considered essential for concentration.

Attitudes toward privacy and noise are perhaps most obviously evident in our libraries. Libraries are no longer silent places for individual study in carrels, though usually areas are reserved for quiet study with no cell phone use. More and more campus libraries are technology hubs and gathering spaces, with food and beverages readily available. They represent in a physical way the changes that have taken place in the way we do research, in terms of both the impact of technology and the increase in collaborative research. For example, the Weigle Information Commons at the University of Pennsylvania is a collaborative teaching effort among the library staff, the College of Arts and Sciences, and the Office of the Provost. The Commons is actually three complementary centers that include technology, digital media, and academic consulting services. The physical facility incorporates collaborative work spaces called alcove areas that include plasma monitors, wireless keyboards, and laptop connections for computer users. Data Diner Booths, group study rooms, and consulting rooms also share similar technology, in addition to three video-recording rooms. One faculty member noted, "I am astonished to see how the space and its services are transforming my teaching and my students as they continue to take greater control of the process and production of knowledge.... My students are becoming scholars" (Yee, 2005, p. 12).

Throughout this book, we have argued that our conceptions of teaching and learning and of curriculum design need to evolve, leaving behind the vestiges of the old paradigm. If we accept the concept of learner-centered institutions and learner-centered curricula that are more collaborative, integrative, flexible, and so on, then we need to consider the physical landscape that supports and reinforces those qualities. In keeping with the pattern we have established, we will begin by looking at the way our physical spaces have been influenced by the instructional paradigm.

The Influence of the Instructional Paradigm on Physical Spaces

If you look online for clipart or photos related to teaching and classrooms, the most common image is that of a room with tablet armchairs all facing the front of the room with a teacher's desk (with an apple on it, of course) in front of a black chalkboard.

This configuration, whether in classrooms or large lecture halls with fixed seating or in lecture halls with ranked rows leading to the focal point where the professor holds forth in the front, made sense when the mode of instruction was one of transferring information from professor to student. In a model where the teacher is the central figure—the sage on the stage—then it only makes sense to have the professor as the central point of interest in the front of the room with a variety of aids for transmitting information—blackboard, overhead projector, television monitors.

This configuration establishes a one-directional communication pattern from professor to student, thus limiting and even discouraging student interaction. White (1990) notes that

> classroom seating patterns are central to the notion of improving communication within the classroom both from a student-teacher standpoint as well as that

between students. Extensive research strongly suggests
that student communication has a direct correlation
with students' placement within the room. (p. 4)

This configuration is reflective of the instructional paradigm, in
which students compete with one another for the approval (aka
grade) of the teacher, who controls the dissemination of knowledge
within the environment where students receive knowledge from the
source of authority. This communication pattern reflects an environment where collaboration is discouraged or even prohibited.

The separation and "ownership" of space is reflective of the silo
effect of the instructional paradigm. In Chapter Two we referred
to the ever-increasing specialization within disciplines that leads to
turf wars. Discipline wars can spill over into allocation of classroom
space too, becoming *turf* wars. At one time we conducted a
classroom space audit in order to determine how effective we were
with space utilization. Each semester when department heads would
develop their schedules, there would be an outcry over needed
classroom space. We knew that there was enough space because
during a renovation project years previously, two of the main
classroom buildings were shut down concurrently for renovation,
yet all classes continued to meet. What we discovered was that
departments were not only refusing to share spaces with others but
were hiding spaces from other units. The problem was not one of
space but of paradigm.

In competitive as opposed to collaborative environments, one's
space or turf represents power, and in an atmosphere where competition predominates, the result is often duplication of space and
equipment. When we discussed in Chapter Two the duplication of
courses that results from territoriality, we used the illustration
of an institution with four different courses on Web design in
three different colleges. In that particular case, each program
owned its computer lab in spite of the fact that two of the
programs were severely undersubscribed. Integration of learning

and collaborative learning experiences for students can—and, we would argue, should—go hand in hand with reconceptualizing the learning spaces that complement those efforts. The more integrated the curriculum becomes, the more necessary it becomes to have spaces that support that integration.

Realigning with the New Paradigm: What the Research Tells Us

In her edited volume *The Importance of Physical Space in Creating Supportive Learning Environments*, Chism (2002) writes, "We know too much about how learning occurs to continue to ignore the ways in which learning spaces are planned, constructed and maintained" (p. 5). We have repeated the point that the learner-centered paradigm is built on recent and emerging research on how people learn. A considerable body of research is also available on how the physical environment affects learning. As we struggle to shift toward a learning-centered academic environment that fosters collaborative, active engagement on the part of the student and a more facilitative role for the professor, our needs in terms of physical spaces must necessarily shift as well. As we expect students to engage in learning activities that take place outside the classroom, we need to consider how space functions to support that goal by reenvisioning the entire campus as a learning space.

In a podcast by SCUP, Flusche (2005a) explored everyday opportunities to enrich students' learning experiences by improving the physical environment. In addition to discussing community spaces, he noted the number of opportunities for learning through landscaping, using examples of outdoor seating areas coupled with historical or artistic expressions. He stated, "Every space, building, office, event, or activity on campus presents an opportunity for the college to be intentionally educational." Although our focus here is primarily on classrooms and gathering spaces, there is much food for thought in his statement and a myriad of opportunities to focus on learning if we begin to think of our campuses in this way.

Visual Elements and Silent Messages

Jensen (1995) examined optimal environments for learning. Visual stimuli are particularly important, as 80 to 90 percent of all information absorbed by the brain is visual. Color is among those visual elements that have a dramatic impact. According to Jensen, "Color has impact because it is part of the spectrum of electromagnetic radiation" (p. 56), and the wavelength of individual colors affects the brain in different ways. Engelbrecht (2003) wrote that "color elicits a total response from human beings because the energy produced by the light that carries color effects [sic] our body functions and influences our mind and emotion" (p. 1). She referred to studies that indicated that color can affect a student's attention span, eye strain, work productivity, and accuracy. Hue is not the only consideration. Intensity and contrast are equally important because studies have shown that monotone environments may induce anxiety and lead to irritability and an inability to concentrate. Thompson (1973, p. 5) wrote that "color is a silent language, a unique and subtle symbol system used by humans, consciously and subconsciously, to send each other information." More research on the effects of color are needed because research to this point indicates that the mental stimulation students and teachers passively receive from the color in a room helps them stay focused. At this time, there is conflicting evidence regarding the effect of hue; however, the need for contrast is well established.

Jensen (1995) also discusses the unconscious effect of items of aesthetic interest, items he labels peripherals. "Peripherals in the form of positive affirmations, learner-generated work, images depicting change, growth, beauty can be powerful vehicles of expression" (p. 59). For example, in the FSU BIS program office, we intentionally chose artwork that depicted images of flight and fancy—an oil painting of a peacock taking flight; a print of a woman flying with a wolf; the horses of the Spanish Riding School doing flying lead changes—along with our program icon, a mobile of road signs pointing somewhere, anywhere, nowhere, there, with one sign labeled *here* pointing down to the guest chair beneath it. The subconscious message we want to send is that with our program, students can take flight to anywhere they choose. The aesthetics of a space affect students' receptivity to ideas and to learning in general.

The visual presentation of the classroom also sends messages to students about learning and how learning will occur in the space. The concept of classroom arrangement having an impact on learning is not new. Numerous researchers (Sommer, 1977; Anderson, 1971; Haney & Zimbardo, 1975; Hennings, 1975) have written about the influence of classroom design on learning. Weinstein and Woolfolk (1981), recognizing the symbolic impact of classroom arrangement, wrote that "the visual appearance of the classroom can be conceptualized as a nonverbal statement about the teacher who has structured this learning environment" (p. 383). Seating arrangement, for example, sends messages about power and control as well as patterns of communication.

We have discussed the role students' prior learning plays in their ability or willingness to learn new things. Prior learning, or perhaps we should say previous experiences in regard to room arrangement, also has an impact on students' expectations about learning. In *Leading the Learner-Centered Campus* (Harris & Cullen, 2010), we discussed three seating arrangements in terms of the social norms students acknowledge and the resulting predisposition toward learning. The three seating options pictured in Figures 8.1, 8.2, and 8.3 send different messages to students regarding their role as learner, and each fosters a different communication pattern in the classroom.

Figure 8.1 features a seating pattern that is familiar to anyone who has gone to church, watched a movie, or attended a public theatrical or comedy performance. The social norm in each of these contexts is to be passive and receptive. It is not surprising then for students to expect to receive information or even to be entertained

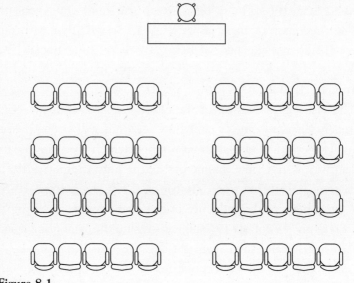

Figure 8.1.

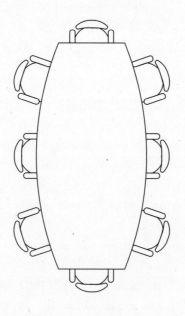

Figure 8.2.

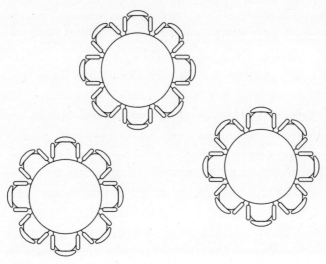

Figure 8.3.

by a performance of some sort when they enter a classroom set up in this manner.

Figure 8.2 features a seminar style seating configuration that exposes the student. Seats arranged in this pattern reduce the student's sense of anonymity, which is characteristic of lecture hall seating where individuals are part of a mass audience. Teachers can hold students more accountable in this setting, as there is no one for the student to hide behind; however, it is not an optimal seating pattern in regard to power and control because the communication pattern is still teacher directed. Prior experiences that contextualize this pattern would include a board room or formal dining room, settings in which a clear hierarchy exists in relation to seating position around the table. Although this arrangement is more conducive to discussion, the teacher still retains power in the pattern of communication.

Figure 8.3 features modular or pod-configuration seating. This pattern increases opportunities for student exchange and reduces the power of the teacher in terms of the communication pattern. Prior experiences that inform this pattern include having a casual meal or playing a board game, situations where individuals sit in small groups expecting to talk with one another. For an individual to sit passively or silently in these social situations is inappropriate and construed as rude by other participants. It is thus not surprising that students expect to participate when they enter a classroom set up in this pattern.

Class size obviously affects one's ability to alter seating patterns. The seminar and pod configurations lend themselves to smaller classes. We acknowledge that the large lecture hall is not going to disappear, but as we noted in the previous chapter, technology can help support learner-centered pedagogy and compensate for large class sizes. Recall the technology-enhanced lecture hall created for the Western PharmD. The designers chose a hexagonal shape in order to reduce the distance between professor and student and employed multiple technologies to foster interaction between professor and student and among students. Later in this chapter, we will describe a model classroom designed by Steelcase that employs technology to overcome the barriers created by the traditional lecture hall.

In the opening of this chapter, we made the point that many instructors make do or find ways to accommodate for less than optimal physical spaces. We have all seen great lecturers who get out from behind the protection of the podium, moving everywhere around the lecture hall and walking up to students when they comment, thus making the large room appear much smaller. It's not that good teaching isn't possible in these spaces; after all, people have been educated well in these settings for many decades. However, given what we now know about learning and considering the changes we are trying to make in our pedagogy, we should try to create optimal environments to support that pedagogy rather than always having to make do or accommodate.

Renovating for Symbolic Impact

In the opening of this chapter, we referred to two volumes produced by SCUP featuring excellence in educational environments. Each year, the *Chronicle of Higher Education* also devotes an issue to new buildings. It is evident from the magnificent projects in these publications that careful planning is taking place in order to create contemporary spaces for learning; and in many cases, institutions have used these projects to demonstrate their commitment to learning and to specific elements of their mission. Building projects, whether new buildings or renovations of existing structures, carry symbolic impact.

In *Leading the Learner-Centered Campus* (Harris & Cullen, 2010), we described a renovation project that was a physical manifestation of a cultural shift that we had initiated. In fact, the renaming of the building alone had tremendous symbolic impact. The original name was the Instructional Resource Center (IRC). The IRC was divided into an instructional wing comprising four large tiered auditoriums and a two-story wing for studios, offices, and other spaces. Built with a focus on *instruction*—delivery of content—the 150- and 200-seat auditoriums were furnished with large, rear projection screens and audiovisual equipment designed to disseminate information to large numbers of students.

The renovated building, which houses the Faculty Center as well as learning spaces that were not tied to any one discipline, was renamed the Interdisciplinary Resource Center (IRC). To achieve the goal of flexible, multidisciplinary spaces, the floors of the auditoriums were flattened to create spaces that could accommodate moveable furnishings. The new classrooms each feature an unusual shape—neither square nor rectangular—that virtually precludes an obvious *front* of the classroom, thus minimizing the dichotomy between teacher and student spaces. The rooms are furnished with tables that feature multiple folding options and chairs with casters to promote ease of movement. Each space is carpeted, comfortable, colorful, and technologically advanced.

To foster learning inside and outside the classroom, spill-out spaces for students were incorporated in the design: private student gathering rooms directly outside the classrooms, and a connector space of approximately six thousand square feet linking the building to the adjacent building and providing a study area and a flexible gathering area.

The interior of the connector space was designed to be a comfortable and aesthetically pleasing work environment, and it has become a very popular gathering space. A post-and-beam system was incorporated, providing an implied boundary within the large open space, which encourages collaboration and supported technology integration, a key component that we will return to in this chapter. One corner of the connector includes white boards and upholstered chairs with tablet arms intended for student group work and collaborative projects. Much to our delight, it has become one of the most used features of the connector space—other than the coffee house.

That project facilitated a strategic step in the process of transforming the campus, both physically and intellectually, away from an instructional focus toward a learner-centered one. Renovation and building projects provide us with the opportunity to make our buildings define, in a corporeal way, our mission of becoming a learning-centered academic environment.

In a similar venture, the University of Iowa renovated its Seamans Center for the Engineering Arts and Sciences to address what it perceived as increasing fragmentation and a disorienting design that resulted from numerous add-on renovations. Designed with the goal of establishing community, the facility has a strategically designed circulation pattern with public gathering areas and two expansive open spaces housing the Student Learning Center and the Student Commons, all of which connect with the university library. The Student Commons is considered to be the living room of the building, with the intent of providing a social focus to the structure; the Student Learning Center is devoted to teamwork, and functions as a collaborative hub for interchange. The symbolic impact of placing the learning center, the commons, and the library at the center of this renovation is obvious.

A community college in Michigan has created an unusual learning space with symbolic impact. Over the past several years, Montcalm Community College has, through donations and grants, recreated an historic village on its campus. The Heritage Village comprises twenty-six buildings, including a railway depot, a law office, a town hall, a church, a doctor's office, and a variety of storefronts. Each is an original building from the county that has been reconstructed on the site, and the village is maintained by local volunteers who act as docents. In addition to using the village as a museum, the college has now begun holding history classes in the buildings, and students conduct research on local figures, whom they later portray in a local reenactment for the public.

This interesting use of space offers students the chance to work together collaboratively while enriching their understanding of their local community and ties with the past. The village carries symbolic value, honoring the history of the locale and hosting numerous activities and learning opportunities for local residents. Even more important is the dedication of campus property to local history, which demonstrates an understanding and commitment to the role of the college in the community.

These projects serve as examples of building renovation incorporating elements to support general learner-centered pedagogy. In the remainder of this chapter, we will consider physical spaces in relation to the specific design elements of learner-centered curricula which we defined in Chapter Three.

Community and Collaboration by Design

Physical spaces can either promote or hinder collaboration and community. O'Banion (1997) makes the point that learning is not limited to the classroom and lab, that it takes place in various formal and informal places. In describing the learner-centered curriculum, we referred to the need for dialogue, for students and faculty to engage in discussion; for through discussion, learning deepens. An important physical feature of the learner-centered campus, then, will be places for those discussions to take place.

Twenty years ago, the FSU campus had very limited spaces for students to gather. Prior to the renovation of the Arts and Sciences Commons building in the mid-1990s, students used to congregate at the end of the hallway on the second floor. There were only a few straight-back chairs that faculty had donated from their offices, but the space was a popular gathering spot between classes—so popular, in fact, that student organizations would sell coffee and doughnuts there to raise funds. As faculty office space demands became critical, that space was converted to temporary faculty offices, and the students had nowhere to go. In the absence of a student union, the loss of this space became an issue of real concern. The student uproar over the loss of a dark corner at the end of a hallway brought to our attention the critical need for student gathering spaces.

When the Arts and Sciences Commons building was renovated, a comfortable atrium provided ample gathering space for students; in addition, small study rooms were incorporated along the classroom hallways. Since that time, a new technology-rich library has become the focal point of student gathering, as has the IRC we described earlier.

Simply providing spaces is the first step. Strategically placed spaces that provide comfortable seating and adequate lighting are essential to creating community. And renovating existing spaces to provide seating is much less expensive than building new spaces. In addition to constructed spaces, as in a student union or coffeehouse, seating in hallways throughout classroom buildings is beneficial. A colleague from another campus described commuter students spending time between classes in their cars. Once space was renovated—in this case the library, which included study rooms, a cyber café, and rooms for small-group meetings—the students literally moved from the parking lot into the library.

On the Indiana University campus at Kokomo, the Virgil and Elizabeth Hunt Hall was designed by BSA LifeStructures around a concept called "soft" spaces, where students and faculty have areas to sit and converse adjacent to teaching spaces. The building houses mathematics and sciences and incorporates classrooms, an advanced technology auditorium, and faculty offices. The design has successfully encouraged people to congregate throughout the building.

Collaboration can be supported in several ways through the design of physical spaces. First, within the classroom, furniture should be easily moved and, if possible, reconfigured. One of our favorite tables is the Herman Miller Butterfly because it features a twelve-inch center base piece with holes for electrical cords, and two drop leaves allowing for numerous reconfigurations. The table is also on casters, allowing for ease of movement. All the tables can be lined up against the wall taking away only one foot of the room's depth or width, and tables can be fit together to create a seminar-style table or different pods of varying sizes. Furniture of this type provides maximum flexibility within the classroom.

Spill-out spaces outside the classroom are also ideal. We incorporated spaces of this sort, both private conference room spaces as well as more open lounge spaces, in our IRC project. Western University also incorporated spill-out spaces adjacent to their state-of-the-art lecture facilities, allowing students to break into groups for projects and find private areas near the classroom to work. San Jose State's Academic Success Center offers another fine example of informal learning spaces coupled with more formal settings. It features what it calls the Incubator Classroom, a classroom setting intended for pedagogical experimentation incorporating various technological tools, collaboration, recording of class work, and informal collaborative areas adjacent to the classroom.

There is probably no academic space more expensive to build and maintain and historically more territorial than laboratory space. Yet today institutions are breaking those barriers and creating collaborative lab spaces. Carnegie Mellon's Doherty Hall incorporates interdisciplinary laboratory spaces. Designed by Burt Hill Kosar Rittelmann Associates, the plan placed major mechanical shafts and ductwork on one edge of the structure in order to provide unobstructed laboratory floor spaces. Casework and fume hoods are positioned to allow for team clusters, and rolling carts provide mobility for chemicals and instrumentation. It is a collaborative space also featuring abundant daylight, so often absent in laboratory settings.

Another elegant example of a collaborative research space is that of the Powell-Focht Bioengineering building at the University of California, San Diego. The four-story building, designed by Anshen and Allen, houses multidisciplinary research in bioengineering. In addition to flexible laboratory spaces, the building contains classrooms and multipurpose lecture halls, and groups faculty offices in suites at the ends of the research wing in order to foster faculty interaction and collaboration.

Perhaps the most outstanding example of design committed to scientific collaboration is Harvard Medical School's New Research Building—ten stories and 740,000 square feet of glass and metal created to foster collaborative research. The structure houses hospital-based and school-based faculty, who share laboratories as well as lounges, discussion areas, conference rooms, and more. These shared spaces support formal as well as casual encounters, increasing the daily interaction of the people who work in the space and thus fostering community as well as collaboration.

Sharing Power

How can the principle of sharing power be applied to the design of learning spaces? Clearly, when we design new spaces, we need to ask students to participate to offer their opinions. Steelcase, one of the leading furniture designers for higher education, has a team that goes out to campuses and, using methodology derived from anthropological research, observes students in their habitat, monitoring their current activities to discover the patterns of use in order to gain a first-hand sense of how students use the campus, gathering spaces, furniture, and so on. They take note, for example, of whether students are using furniture in the way it was intended. When they visited our campus, we were surprised to learn that the upholstered benches that we provided in one study area were not used for additional seating or as coffee-table-type work areas as they were intended. The students either dragged them to a corner and used them for sleeping, or used them as storage areas, piling their bags and coats on them. The Steelcase team also conducts extensive interviews with students in the settings they monitor. As a result of the visit to our campus, they made suggestions regarding storage options so that students could safely stow some of the many belongings they carry with them every day. The inclusion of student opinion is an important first step.

Steelcase has also developed a prototype classroom that is being piloted by Grand Valley State University, a room that the company claims breaks the mold of cinderblock classrooms. The Steelcase University Learning Center (SULC) incorporates collaborative zones with white boards and offers what the company calls multiple stages as opposed to a single dissemination point. In other words, there is no teacher front, or what Steelcase calls *teacher wall*. White boards and projection screens completely line the room, and small group tables are angled in a star pattern, allowing view of projected material from any point in the room. It is, of course, technology rich, including power sources in the tables, and webcams that capture notes written on white boards. The room is designed to accommodate multiple learning styles. The two words Steelcase uses to describe the room are *connection* and *choice*, both features of the learner-centered curriculum.

In fairness we should also mention that Steelcase's major competitor, Herman Miller, has also partnered with a number of universities in its Learning Studio Research program. The innovative spaces Herman Miller has designed align with several principles, all learner-centered in theory. Its educational solutions, which it markets as a formula of people + pedagogy + place, are designed around six key adjectives: adaptable, social, stimulating, healthful, resourceful, and sustainable. Its design solutions include rooms with flexible furniture, multiple work surfaces, high-end technology, lots of available power, aesthetically pleasing furnishings, and design elements that can be moved and reconfigured to meet pedagogical needs.

Low-Cost Options

Of course, not everyone is going to be able to afford multiple classrooms, or even one classroom, of this type, but there are other, less expensive options for offering students connection and choice. Sometimes, letting students take charge ends up yielding greater results for less money. We experienced this when we were struggling to find a space for graphic arts students to use as a twenty-four-hour lab space. We had a serious problem with students spraying fixatives on their work in unsafe places in the residential areas. So we decided to designate a residence hall for graphic arts students and to provide a lab space on the lower floor with a spray box for the safe handling of fixatives. As we struggled to meet various ADA and health and fire code requirements for residential facilities, we found that the cost of installing the spray box ate up the majority of the funds available.

At first we thought we would have to abandon the project, but one of the faculty members from the program assured us that if we simply got some old tables from storage and allowed the students to paint and design the space themselves, the students would be happy. The students did a fantastic job of creating a lively, colorful space for work that also demonstrated their growing design expertise—positive peripherals of their own design. Aside from the financing of the spray box, the project cost was minimal. The students loved their lab space and took ownership of it with pride, a perfect example of people supporting what they help build.

In a similar gesture of sharing power, the College of Technology at another institution was able to do some renovation and took the occasion to engage its students of architecture. The students were encouraged to enter their design for the space in a contest. The winner had the opportunity to work as an intern with the architectural firm hired for the project, working with professionals to make any necessary adaptations to the submitted plan. The student who won not only had his design used for the project but also was hired by the architectural firm upon graduation.

Displaying student work is also a means of sharing power and of equipping the environment with positive peripherals. Typical ways of doing this are gallery shows of student work, public presentations of capstone projects, or public presentations of display boards. Because we have minimal physical presence on the FSU campus, one way that we have used to display work for the BIS is to post student essays to our Web site. The first assignment that they write in the orientation course is called "The Road to the BIS," and in that paper, students reflect on their academic and nonacademic learning adventure that has led them to the BIS. The stories are rich and varied, and posting them to the Web site serves a dual purpose: honoring those students who are asked and providing great public relations and marketing for the program.

Flusche (2005b), writing for SCUP, posed the question of whether institutions celebrate the work of students, whether student learning is truly a prominent value of the institution.

> Are student art works, demonstration projects or research papers readily available in the student center, library or in building entranceways? Is faculty work easily found—their publications, inventions, or personal hobbies? Are notable alumni visibly held up as role models for future generations through Walls of Honor or other ongoing modes of recognition? (p. 1)

In assessing institutional messages regarding student learning as a central value, he asks,

> Are the classrooms, laboratories, studio and library the best maintained, equipped and comfortable spaces on campus? Do campus policies such as quiet hours and the provision of study spaces encourage serious academic work? Do academic departments welcome students and facilitate faculty-student contact? Do offices post pictures of members of the faculty, staff, administration so that student will recognize them by [sight]? (p. 2)

These are all valuable questions to consider, as they raise institutional awareness of unstated and perhaps unintentional messages that schools may send in regard to student learning and the value of student and faculty work.

Chapter Summary

In this chapter, we raised the issue of physical spaces as they affect learning. Campuses across the country are experimenting with classroom and building design that supports a learner-centered environment: rooms that are technologically state-of-the-art; rooms that take into account multiple means of teaching and learning; rooms that can morph into multiple configurations for any given learning experience, accompanied by spaces that support collaboration, dialogue, and exchange. In regard to curriculum design, we emphasized the need for spaces that support community and that support the sharing of power with students, and we offered a variety of examples, some at little cost, that can begin to address both community and power sharing. As we continue our efforts to create learner-centered institutions, physical manifestations of those efforts serve as constant reminders of our purposes and intentions. We should try to remain aware of the silent messages that physical spaces or configurations of space send, and to ensure that those messages are congruent with our purposes. Learner-centeredness is reflected everywhere on campus—by leadership, by curriculum, and by campus design and facilities.

Closing Thoughts

Although learner-centered practices are being employed with great success by many teachers in individual classrooms, not much attention has been paid to how those experiences could or should be linked together. These efforts need to be supported through curriculum design. Curriculum is the heart of what we do. It needs to be examined and to be aligned with learner-centered practices if our institutions are going to become truly learner-centered. In this book, we examined curriculum design from the vantage point of a postmodern, learner-centered perspective.

We began by posing the question, *Why do we need to redesign curriculum?* Our answer was that learner-centered curricula provide opportunities for our graduates to become creative, autonomous learners, the people most needed in the twenty-first-century workforce. We then examined curriculum as it manifested itself in the modern era—that is, the instructional paradigm—in order to identify assumptions about curriculum that we have accepted as facts, or as we put it, the unexamined reality of our paradigm. We followed that discussion with a new way of looking at curriculum, a postmodern way that challenges assumptions predicated on a modern view of learning and education. Recognizing that implementing these kinds of changes will be challenging, we offered strategies for implementation, suggesting a rhetorical strategy for leaders to employ that itself is postmodern by design. To illustrate that these postmodern, learner-centered design principles are not just theoretical constructs but very real options, we provided examples of curricula that vary in degree of learner-centeredness and a rubric for assessing the degree of learner-centeredness in a curriculum. We discussed practical ways of supporting learner-centered curricula, through assessment practices, use of technology, and consideration of physical space.

We believe that the curriculum, whether institutional or programmatic, needs to be redesigned. Individual instructors employing learner-centered practices in their individual classrooms have greatly increased our understanding of what we mean by learner-centered, but for the paradigmatic shift to be fully realized, all of us need to look beyond what takes place in individual classrooms and consider how those experiences link to and inform one another.

In Chapter One we asserted that the twenty-first century is dependent on autonomous learners who can be creative and inno-vative. The minds needed to cultivate the future must be trained in multiple disciplines. They must be creative, for "individuals with-out creating capacities will be replaced by computers and will drive away those who do have the creative spark" (Gardner, 2008, p. 18). We believe that the research that informs the learner-centered agenda offers us the opportunity to create learning environments to foster these qualities in learners, by placing learning and the learner at the center of focus. To quote Gardner, "The survival and thriving of our species will depend on our nurturing of potentials that are distinctly human" (p. 167). It is the focus on learning as a distinctly human activity that characterizes learner-centeredness.

We envision this book as a catalyst for thinking about curricu-lum design. We believe that learning is the result of continuous discussion and reflection. That is how the process of curriculum redesign should also begin, and what we have offered here are some of the topics of conversation to stimulate that process.

References

Alexander, B. (2008, July-August). Games for higher education: 2008. *EDU-CAUSE Review, 43*(4). www.educause.edu/EDUCAUSE+Review/EDUCAUSE ReviewMagazineVolume43/GamesforHigherEducation2008/163066.

Allen, M. J. (2004). *Assessing academic programs in higher education*. San Francisco: Jossey-Bass.

Amabile, T. M. (1996). *Creativity in context: Update to the social psychology of creativity*. Boulder, CO: Westview Press.

American Association of Colleges of Pharmacy. (2006). Roadmap to 2015: Preparing competent pharmacists and pharmacy faculty for the future. Combined report of the 2005–06 Argus commission and the academic affairs, professional affairs and research and graduate affairs committees. *American Journal of Pharmaceutical Education, 70*(5), 1–27.

American Association of University Professors. (2008). *The annual report on the economic status of the profession, 2007–08*. www.aaup.org/AAUP/pubsres /academe/2008/MA/sal/sal.htm.

American Psychological Association. (2008). *Learner-centered psychological principles*. www.apa.org/ed/governance/bea/learner-centered.pdf.

Anderson, R. (1971). The school as an organic teaching aid. In R. M. McClure (Ed.), *National society for the study of education yearbook: Part 1. The curriculum: Retrospect and prospect* (pp. 271–306). Chicago: University of Chicago Press.

Angelo, T., & Cross, P. (1993). *Classroom assessments techniques: A handbook for college teachers*. San Francisco: Jossey-Bass.

Association of American Colleges and Universities. (2002). *Greater expectations: A new vision for learning as a nation goes to college*. Washington, DC: Author.

Association of American Colleges and Universities. (2004). *Statement on integrative learning*. www.aacu.org/integrative_learning/pdfs/ILP_Statement.pdf.

Bandura, A. (1986). *Social foundations of thought and action*. Upper Saddle River, NJ: Prentice Hall.

Bandura, A. (1993). Perceived self-efficacy in cognitive development and functioning. *Educational Psychologist, 28*, 117–148.

Bandura, A. (1994). Self-efficacy. In V. S. Ramachaudran (Ed.), *Encyclopedia of human behavior* (Vol. 4, pp. 71–81). New York: Academic Press.

Bandura, A. (1997). *Self-efficacy: The exercise of control*. New York: Freeman.

Banta, T. W., Jones, E. A., & Black, K. E. (2009). *Designing effective assessment: Principles and profiles of good practice*. San Francisco: Jossey-Bass.

Barr, R., & Tagg, J. (1995). From teaching to learning: A new paradigm for undergraduate education. *Change, 27*(6), 13–25.

Barrett, H. C. (2004). Electronic portfolios as digital stories of deep learning. http://electronicportfolios.org/digistory/epstory.html.

Beane, J. A. (1995). Curriculum integration and the disciplines of knowledge. *Phi Delta Kappan, 76*, 616–626.

Beane, J. A. (1997). Curriculum integration: Designing the core of democratic education. New York: Columbia University Press.

Beatty, I. (2004, February 3). Transforming student learning with classroom communication systems. *Research Bulletin* [EDUCAUSE Center for Applied Research], no. 3. http://arxiv.org/pdf/physics/0508129.

Beauchamp, G. A. (1975). *Curriculum theory* (3rd ed.). Wilmette, IL: Kagg Press.

Bernstein, B. (1971). On the classification and framing of educational knowledge. In M. Young (Ed.), *Knowledge and control: New directions for the sociology of education* (pp. 47–69). London: Macmillan.

Bernstein, B. (1990). *Class codes and control: Vol. 4. The structuring of academic discourse*. London: Routledge.

Bernstein, B. (1996). *Pedagogy, symbolic control and identity: Theory, research, critique*. London: Taylor & Francis.

Bernstein, B. (2000). *Pedagogy, symbolic control, and identity: Theory, research, critique* (Rev. ed.). Lanham, MD: Rowman & Littlefield.

Biggs, J. B. (1987). *Student approaches to learning and studying*. Australian Council for Educational Research, Hawthorn, Victoria.

Biggs, J. B. (2003). *Teaching for quality learning at university*. Buckingham, England: Open University.

Blumberg, P. (2008). *Developing learner-centered teaching: A practical guide for faculty*. San Francisco: Jossey-Bass.

Bobbitt, F. (1918). *The curriculum*. Boston: Riverside Press.

Bobbitt, F. (1924). *How to make a curriculum*. New York: Houghton Mifflin.

Boggs, G. R., & Michael, D. G. (1997). The Palomar college experience. In T. O'Banion, *A learning college for the 21st century* (pp. 189–210). Phoenix, AZ: American Council on Education/Oryx Press.

Bowden, J., & Martin, F. (1998). *The university of learning*. London: Kogan Page.

Bransford, J. D., Brown, A. L., & Cocking, R. R. (2000). Learning: From speculation to science. In J. D. Bransford, A. L. Brown, & R. R. Cockin (Eds.), *How people learn: Brain, mind, experience, and school* (pp. 3–27). Washington, DC: National Academies Press.

Bridges, W. (1994). *Job shift: How to prosper in a workplace without jobs*. Cambridge, MA: Perseus Press.

Bronson, P., & Merryman, A. (2010, July 10). The creativity crisis. *Newsweek*. www.newsweek.com/2010/07/10/the-creativity-crisis.html.

Brookfield, S. (1995). *Becoming a critically reflective teacher*. San Francisco: Jossey-Bass.

Bruffee, K. A. (1995). A nonfoundational curriculum. In J. G. Haworth & C. F. Conrad (Eds.), *Revisioning curriculum in higher education* (pp. 26–34). Needham Heights, MA: Simon & Schuster.

Bruner, J. (1960). *The process of education*. Cambridge, MA: Harvard University Press.

Bruner, J. (1996). *The culture of education*. Cambridge, MA: Harvard University Press.

Bunce, D. M., VandenPlas, J. R., & Havanki, K. L. (2006). Comparing the effectiveness on student achievement of a student response system versus online webCT quizzes. *Journal of Chemical Education, 83*(3), 488.

Burkhardt, P. (2006). Administering interdisciplinary and innovative programs: Lessons from the rise and fall of Arizona International College. *Issues in Integrative Studies, 24*(1), 159–172.

Candy, P. C. (1991). *Self-direction for lifelong learning: A comprehensive guide to theory and practice*. San Francisco: Jossey-Bass.

Carrithers, D., & Bean, J. C. (2008). Using a client memo to assess critical thinking of finance majors. *Business Communication Quarterly, 71*(1), 10–26.

Chism, N.V.N. (2002). A tale of two classrooms. In N.V.N. Chism & D. Bickford (Eds.), *The importance of physical space in creating supportive learning environments* (pp. 5–11). New Directions for Teaching and Learning, no. 92. San Francisco: Jossey-Bass.

Colley, S. L. (2009). *Nursing faculty experiences and perceptions of the implementation process to a learner-centered teaching philosophy: A case study*. Unpublished doctoral dissertation, Western Michigan University.

Conway, M., Perfect, T., Anderson, W., Gardiner, J., & Cohen, G. (1997). Changes in memory awareness during learning: The acquisition of knowledge by psychology undergraduates. *Journal of Experimental Psychology: General, 126*, 393–413.

Covington, M. (1992). *Making the grade: Self-worth perspective on motivation and school reform*. New York: Cambridge University Press.

Csikszentmihalyi, M. (1990). *Flow: The psychology of optimal experience*. New York: Harper and Row.

Csikszentmihalyi, M. (1996). *Creativity*. New York: HarperCollins.

Csikszentmihalyi, M. (1999). Implications of a systems perspective for the study of creativity. In R. Sternberg (Ed.), *Handbook of creativity* (pp. 337–349). New York: Cambridge University.

Deci, E., Nezlec, J., & Sheinomy, L. (1981). Characteristics of the rewarder. *Journal of Personality and Social Psychology, 40*, 1–10.

Derting, T. L., & Ebert-May, D. (2010). Learner-centered inquiry in undergraduate biology: Positive relationships with long-term student achievement. *CBE—Life Sciences Education, 40*, 462–472.

Dewey, J. (1956). *The child and the curriculum*. Chicago: University of Chicago Press.

DeZure, D., Babb, M., & Waldmann, S. (2005). Integrative learning nationwide: Emerging themes and practices. *Peer Review, 7*(3), 24–28.

Diaz, A. J., Middendorf, J., Pace, D., & Shopkow, L. (2008). The history learning project: A department decodes its students. *Journal of American History, 94*, 1211–1224.

Doll, W. E., Jr. (1993). *A post-modern perspective on curriculum*. New York: Teachers College Press.

Doll, W. E., Jr. (1995). Curriculum possibilities in a "post"-future. In J. G. Haworth & C. F. Conrad (Eds.), *Revisioning curriculum in higher education* (pp. 58–69). Needham Heights, MA: Simon & Schuster.

Doll, W. E., Jr. (2002). Ghosts and the curriculum. In W. E. Doll Jr. & N. Gough (Eds.), *Curriculum visions* (pp. 23–70). New York: Lang.

Doll, W. E., Jr., & Gough, N. (Eds.). (2002). *Curriculum visions*. New York: Lang.

Doyle, T. (2008). *Helping students learn in a learner-centered environment: A guide to teaching in higher education*. Sterling, VA: Stylus.

Driscoll, J. W. (1978). Trust and participation in organizational decision making as predictors of satisfaction. *Academy of Management Journal, 21*, 44–56.

Dweck, C. (2000). *Self-theories: Their role in motivation, personality, and development*. Philadelphia: Psychology Press.

Dweck, C. (2006). *Mindsets: The new psychology of success*. New York: Random House.

Dweck, C., & Leggett, E. L. (1988). A social-cognitive approach to motivation and personality. *Psychological Review, 95*, 256–272.

Dweck, C., & Licht, B. G. (1980). Learned helplessness and intellectual achievement. In M.E.P. Seligman & J. Garber (Eds.), *Human helplessness: Theory and application* (pp. 197–221). New York: Academic Press.

Elsner, P. A. (1997). Becoming a learner-centered college system at Maricopa. In T. O'Banion, *A learning college for the 21st century* (pp. 167–188). Phoenix, AZ: American Council on Education/Oryx Press.

Emig, J. (1977). Writing as a mode of learning. *College Composition and Communication, 21*(2), 122–128.

Englebrecht, K. (2003, June 18). *The impact of color on learning*. Presentation at NeoCon 2003. www.coe.uga.edu/sdpl/HTML/W305.pdf.

Entwistle, N. J. (1981). *Styles of learning and teaching: An integrated outline of educational psychology for students, teachers, and lecturers*. Chichester, England: Wiley.

Entwistle, N. J., & Entwistle, A. (1991). Contrasting forms of understanding for degree examinations: The student experience and its implications. *Higher Education, 22*, 205–227.

Entwistle, N. J., & Ramsden, P. (1983). *Understanding student learning*. London: Croom Helm.

Feldman, D. H., Czikszentmihalyi, M., & Gardner, H. (1994). *Changing the world: A framework for the study of creativity*. Westport, CT: Praeger.

Fink, L. D. (2003). *Creating significant learning experiences: An integrated approach to designing college classes*. San Francisco: Jossey-Bass.

Fisher, T. (2007, February 23). Roundtable discussion of campus architecture. *Chronicle of Higher Education*, pp. 38–39.

Florida, R. (2010, March). How the crash will reshape America. *Atlantic*. www.theatlantic.com/magazine/archive/2009/03/how-the-crash-will-reshape-america/7293/.

Flusche, M. (2005a, February). *The intentional campus: Everyday opportunities to enrich students' experiences by improving the physical environment of a college*. Society for College and University Planning webcast. (Available for purchase at www.scup.org/page/profdev/archive-cds/tic.)

Flusche, M. (2005b, November-December). The teaching campus: The unstated messages. *Perspectives on Campus Planning*, no. 12. www.dlca.com/newsletter/newsletter12.html#article3.

Franken, R. E. (2006). *Human motivation* (3rd ed.). Belmont, CA: Wadsworth.

Fuchsman, K. (2007, November 2). Disciplinary realities and interdisciplinary prospects. *Global Spiral*. www.metanexus.net/magazine/tabid/68/id/10192/Default.aspx.

Gaff, J. G. (2004). Editor's notes. In J. L. Ratcliff, D. K. Johnson, & J. G. Gaff (Eds.), *Changing general education curriculum* (pp. 1–8). New Directions for Higher Education, no. 125. San Francisco: Jossey-Bass.

Garavalia, L. S., & Gredler, M. E. (2002). Prior achievement, aptitude, and use of learning strategies as predictors of college student achievement in college. *Student Journal, 36*, 616–625.

Gardner, H. (1983). *Frames of mind: The theory of multiple intelligences*. New York: Basic Books.

Gardner, H. (2006). *Multiple intelligences*. New York: Basic Books.

Gardner, H. (2008). *Five minds for the future*. Boston: Harvard Business Press.

Glenn, D. (2010, September 7). Assessment projects from hell. *Chronicle of Higher Education*. http://chronicle.com/blogs/measuring/assessment-projects -from-hell/26733.

Hackel, M. D. (Ed.). (2002). *Applying the science of learning to university teaching and beyond*. New Directions for Teaching and Learning, no. 89. San Francisco: Jossey-Bass.

Haney, C., & Zimbardo, P. G. (1975, June). It's tough to tell a high school from a prison. *Psychology Today*, pp. 26–36.

Harris, M., & Cullen, R. (2010). *Leading the learner-centered campus: An administrator's framework for improving student learning outcomes*. San Francisco: Jossey-Bass.

Hennings, D. G. (1975). *Mastering classroom communication—What interaction analysis tells the teacher*. Pacific Palisades, CA: Goodyear.

Henry, S. (2005). Disciplinary hegemony meets interdisciplinary ascendancy. *Issues in Integrative Studies*, 23(1), 1–37.

Higher Education Research Institute. (2011). 2011 CIRP freshman survey. www.heri.ucla.edu/cirpoverview.php.

Huba, M. E., & Freed, J. E. (2000). *Learner-centered assessment on college campuses*. Needham Heights, MA: Allyn & Bacon.

Hunkins, F. P., & Hammill, P. A. (1995). Beyond Tyler and Taba: Reconceptualizing the curriculum process. In J. G. Haworth & C. F. (Eds.), *Revisioning curriculum in higher education* (pp. 16–25). Needham Heights, MA: Simon & Schuster.

Hunt, T. C., Lasley, T. J., II, & Raisch, C. D. (2010). *Encyclopedia of educational reform and dissent* (Vol. 1). Thousand Oaks, CA: Sage.

Hutchings, P. (2010). Opening doors to faculty involvement in assessment. Occasional Paper no. 4, National Institute for Learning Outcomes Assessment. www.learningoutcomeassessment.org/documents/PatHutchings_000.pdf.

IBM Global Services. (2008). *Unlocking the DNA of the adaptable workforce: The global human capital study 2008*. http://www-935.ibm.com/services/us/gbs/bus /html/2008ghcs.html.

Jencks, C. (Ed.). (1992). *The postmodern reader*. New York: St. Martin's Press.

Jensen, E. (1995). *Brain-based learning*. San Diego, CA: Brain Store.

Johnson, L., Smith, R., Willis, H., Levine, A., & Haywood, K. (2011). *The Horizon Report (2011 Edition)*. Austin, TX: New Media Consortium.

Jones, E. A. (2002). *Transforming the curriculum: Preparing students for a changing world: ASHE-ERIC Higher Education Report, 29*(3). San Francisco: Jossey-Bass.

Judson, E., & Sawada, A. (2002). Learning from past and present: Electronic response systems in college lecture halls. *Journal of Computers in Mathematics and Science Teaching, 21*(2), 167–181.

Katz, S. N. (2010, September-October). Beyond crude measurement and consumerism. *Academe Online*. www.aaup.org/AAUP/pubsres/academe/2010/SO /feat/katz.htm.

Kelly, R. (2009, September 16). Designing effective assessments: Q&A with Trudy Banta. *Faculty Focus*. www.facultyfocus.com/articles/educational -assessment/designing-effective-assessments-qa-with-trudy-banta/.

Klein, J. T. (2005). Integrative learning and interdisciplinary studies. *Peer Review, 7*(3), 8–10.

Kliewer, J. R. (1999). *The innovative campus: Nurturing the distinctive learning environment*. Phoenix, AZ: Oryx Press.

Knowles, M. (1975). *Self-directed learning*. Chicago: Follet.

Langer, E. (1989). *Mindfulness*. Reading, MA: Addison Wesley.

Langer, E. (1997). *The power of mindful learning*. Reading, MA: Addison Wesley.

Langer, J. A., & Applebee, A. N. (1987). *How writing shapes thinking: A study of teaching and learning*. Urbana, IL: National Council of Teachers of English.

Lattuca, L., & Stark, J. (2009). *Shaping the college curriculum: Academic plans in context*. San Francisco: Jossey-Bass.

Leamnson, R. (1999). *Thinking about teaching and learning: Developing habits of learning with first-year college and university students*. Sterling, VA: Stylus.

Levine, A. (1980). *Why innovation fails*. Albany: State University of New York Press.

Light, R. (2001). *Making the most of college: Students speak their minds*. Boston: Harvard University Press.

Marcell, M. (2005, August). *Effectiveness of online quizzing in increasing class preparation and participation*. Poster presented at the annual meeting of the American Psychological Association, Washington, DC.

Marton, F., Hounsell, D., & Entwistle, N. J. (1977). *The experiments of learning: Implications for teaching and studying in higher education* (2nd ed.). Edinburgh: Scottish Academic Press.

Marton, F., & Säljö, R. (1976). On qualitative differences in learning: Outcome as a function of the learner's conception of the task. *British Journal of Educational Psychology, 46*, 115–127.

Martsolf, D. S., Dieckman, B. C., Cartechine, K. A., Starr, P. J., Wolf, L. E., & Anaya, E. R. (1999). Peer review of teaching: Instituting a program in a college of nursing. *Journal of Nursing Education, 38*, 326–332.

McCombs, B. L. (1989). Self-regulated learning and academic achievement: A phenomenological view. In B. J. Zimmerman & D. H. Schunk (Eds.), *Self-regulated learning and academic achievement: Theoretical perspectives* (pp. 67–124). Hillsdale, NJ: Erlbaum.

McCombs, B. L. (2001). The learner-centered framework: Bringing the educational system into balance. *Educational Horizons, 79*, 182–193.

McConnell, D. (2006). *E-learning groups and communities*. New York: Society for Research into Higher Education and Open University Press.

Mezirow, J. (1991). *Learning as transformation*. San Francisco: Jossey-Bass.

Miller, M. (2009). What the science of cognition tells us about instructional technology. *Change, 42*(3), 16–17.

Moran, M. (2005). *Interdisciplinarity*. London: Routledge.

Moskus, J. (1997). Lane changes: Transformation at Lane Community College. In T. O'Banion, *A learning college for the 21st century* (pp. 150–166). Phoenix, AZ: American Council on Education/Oryx Press.

Mosteller, F. (1989, April). The muddiest point in the lecture. *Journal of the Harvard-Danforth Center, 3*, 1–21.

National Leadership Council for Liberal Education and America's Promise. (2007). *College learning for the new global century: A report from the National Leadership Council for Liberal Education & America's Promise*. Washington, DC: Association of American Colleges and Universities.

National League for Nursing. (2006). About the NLN. www.nln.org/excellence /model/index.htm.

Newell, G. (1984). Learning from writing in two content areas: A study/protocol analysis of writing to learn. *Research in the Teaching of English, 18*, 265–287.

Nygren, K. (2007). Elevating knowledge from level 1 to level 3. In S. W. Beyerlein, C. Holmes, & D. Apple (Eds.), *Faculty guidebook: A comprehensive tool for improving faculty performance* (pp. 165–168). Lisle, IL: Pacific Crest.

O'Banion, T. (1997). *A learning college for the 21st century*. Phoenix, AZ: American Council on Education/Oryx Press.

Oblinger, D. (Ed.). (2000). *Learning spaces: An EDUCAUSE e-book*. www.educause.edu/LearningSpaces/10569.

Pink, D. (2011). *Drive: The surprising truth about what motivates us*. New York: Riverhead Books.

Plucker, M. (2008, October 24). *A 100 year review of creativity research*. Paper presented at the International Creativity Education Conference, Ksionong, Taiwan.

Posner, G. J., Strike, K. A., Hewson, P. W., & Gertzog, W. A. (1982). Accommodation of a scientific conception: Toward a theory of conceptual change. *Science Education, 66*, 211–227.

Prados, J. (Ed.). (1991). *The proud legacy of quality assurance in the preparation of technical professionals: ABET 75th anniversary retrospective*. Baltimore, MD: Accreditation Board for Engineering and Technology.

Prosser, M., & Miller, R. (1989). The "how" and "why" of learning physics. *European Journal of Psychology of Education, 4*, 513–528.

Ramsden, P. (1988). *Improving learning: New perspectives*. London: Kogan Page.

Ramsden, P. (1992). *Learning to teach in higher education*. New York: Routledge.

Ramsden, P. (2003). *Learning to teach in higher education*. London: Routledge-Falmer.

Rogers, C. (1980). *A way of being*. Boston: Houghton Mifflin.

Rogers, S., Booth, M., & Eveline, J. (2003). The politics of disciplinary advantage. *History of Intellectual Culture, 3*(1). www.ucalgary.ca/hic/website /2003vol3no1/framesets/2003vol3no1rodgersarticleframeset.htm.

Rosenthal, R., Baratz, S. S., & Hall, C. M. (1974). Teacher behavior, teacher expectations, and gains in pupils' rated creativity. *Journal of Genetic Psychology, 124*, 115–121.

Ryan, M. R., & Campa, H., III. (2000). Application of learner-based teaching innovations to enhance education in wildlife conservation. *Wildlife Society Bulletin, 28*, 168–179.

Schaefer, K. M., & Zygmont, D. (2003). Analyzing the teaching style of nursing faculty: Does it promote a student-centered or teacher-centered learning environment? *Nursing Education Perspectives 24*, 238–245.

Schapiro, S. R., & Livingstone, J. A. (2000). Dynamic self-regulation: The driving force behind academic achievement. *Innovative Higher Education, 25*(1), 59–76.

Schiro, M. S. (2008). *Curriculum theory: Conflicting visions and enduring concerns*. Thousand Oaks, CA: Sage.

Schön, D. (1983). *The reflective practitioner*. London: Temple Smith.

Scott, D. (2008). *Critical essays on major curriculum theorists*. London: Routledge.

Senor, D., & Singer, S. (2009). *Start-up nation: The story of Israel's economic miracle*. New York: Twelve.

Shaughnessey, M. (1977). *Errors and expectations*. New York: Oxford University Press.

Shenk, D. (2010). *The genius in all of us: Why everything you've been told about genetics, talent, and IQ is wrong*. New York: Doubleday.

Smith, P., Masterson, A., Basford, L., Boddy, G., Costello, S., Marvell, G., Redding, M., & Wallis, B. (2000). Action research: A suitable method for promoting change in nurse education. *Nurse Education Today, 20*, 563–570.

Smith, S. D., & Caruso, J. B. (2010). *The ECAR study of undergraduate students and information technology, 2010*. Boulder, CO: EDUCAUSE.

Sommer, R. (1977). Classroom layout. *Theory into Practice, 16*(3), 6–7.

Stead, D. R. (2005, July). A review of the one-minute paper. *Active Learning in Higher Education, 6*, 118–131.

Sum, P. E., & Light, S. A. (2010). Assessing student learning outcomes and documenting success through a capstone course. *PS: Political Science and Politics, 43*, 523–531.

Svinicki, M. D. (2004). *Learning and motivation in the postsecondary classroom*. Bolton, MA: Anker.

Sylwester, R. (1995). *A celebration of neurons: An educator's guide to the human brain*. Alexandria, VA: Association for Supervision and Curriculum Development.

Tagg, J. (2003). *The learning paradigm college*. Bolton, MA: Anker.

Tierney, W. G. (1995). Cultural politics and the curriculum in postsecondary education. In J. G. Haworth & C. F. Conrad (Eds.), *Revisioning curriculum in higher education* (pp. 35–47). Needham Heights, MA: Simon & Schuster.

Thompson, J. (1973). *Beyond words: Nonverbal communication in the classroom.* New York: Citation Press.

Twigg, C. (2003). *Improving learning and reducing costs: Lessons learned from round 1 of the Pew Grant Program in course redesign.* Troy, NY: Academic Transformation.

Tyler, R. (1949). *Basic principles of curriculum and instruction.* Chicago: University of Chicago Press.

Usher, R., & Edwards, R. (1997). *Postmodernism and education.* London: Routledge.

Volkwein, J. F., Lattuca, L. R., Terenzini, P. T., Strauss, L. C., & Sukhbaatar, J. (2004). Engineering change: A study of the impact of EC2000. *International Journal of Engineering Education, 20,* 318–328.

von Glaserfeld, E. (1995). Constructivist approaches to science teaching. In L. P. Steffe & J. Gale (Eds.), *Constructivism in education* (pp. 3–15). Hillsdale, NJ: Erlbaum.

Wasserman, J., & Beyerlein, S. W. (2007). SII method for assessment reporting. In S. W. Beyerlein, C. Holmes, & D. K. Apple (Eds.), *Faculty guidebook: A comprehensive tool for improving faculty performance* (4th ed., pp. 465–466). Lisle, IL: Pacific Crest.

Weigel, V. B. (2002). *Deep learning for a digital age: Technology's untapped potential to enrich higher education.* San Francisco: Jossey-Bass.

Weimer, M. (2002). *Learner-centered teaching: Five key changes in practice.* San Francisco: Jossey-Bass.

Weimer, M. (2010). *Inspired college teaching: A career-long resource for professional growth.* San Francisco: Jossey-Bass.

Weinstein, C. S., & Woolfolk, A. E. (1981). Classroom design and impression formation: A new area for research. *Contemporary Educational Psychology, 6*, 383–386.

West, J. A., & West, M. L. (2009). *Using wikis for online collaboration: The power of the read-write web.* San Francisco: Jossey-Bass.

White, E. K. (1990). Psychological aspects of classroom planning. *CEPPI's Educational Facility Planner, 28*(5), 4–6.

White, J. (1982). *The aims of education revisited.* London: Routledge & Kegan Paul.

Wigfield, A. L., & Eccles, J. S. (2000). Expectancy-value theory of achievement motivation. *Contemporary Educational Psychology, 25*, 68–81.

Wiggins, G., & McTighe, J. (2005). *Understanding by design* (2nd ed.). Alexandria, VA: Association for Supervision and Curriculum Development.

Wilen-Daugenti, T. (2009). *.edu: Technology and learning environments in higher education.* New York: Lang.

Willingham, D. (2009). *Why don't students like school: A cognitive scientist answers questions about how the mind works and what it means for the classroom.* San Francisco: Jossey-Bass.

Wingspread Group on Higher Education. (1993). *An American imperative: Higher expectations for higher education.* Racine, WI: Johnson Foundation.

Yearwood, E., Singleton, J., Feldman, H. R., & Colombraro, G. (2001). A case study in implementing CQI in a nursing education program. *Journal of Professional Nursing, 17*, 297–304.

Yee, R. (2005). *Educational environments.* New York: Visual Reference Publications.

Young, R. E., Becker, A. L., & Pike, K. L. (1974). *Rhetoric: Discovery and change.* New York: Harcourt, Brace and World.

Zimmerman, B. J. (2002, Spring). Becoming a self-regulated learner: An overview. *Theory into Practice, 41*(2), 64–70.

Zimmerman, B. J., & Schunk, D. H. (Eds.). (1994). *Self-regulation of learning and performance: Issues and educational applications.* Hillsdale, NJ: Erlbaum.

Zull, J. (2002). *The art of changing the brain: Enriching the practice of teaching by exploring the biology of learning.* Sterling, VA: Stylus.

Index

Page references followed by *fig* indicate an illustrated figure; followed by *t* indicate a table.

Course descriptions: learner-center approach to writing, 96–97; traditional approach to, 96

Course management systems (CMSs), 164, 165, 170–171, 180

Covington, M., 36

Creating Significant Learning Experiences: An Integrated Approach to Designing College Classes (Fink), 84

Creative people: failure response by, 17–18; power of choice and opportunities taken by, 18–21

Creative thinking: divergent and convergent modes of, 11; left-brain and right-brain activity during, 10–11; three elements in interaction resulting in, 10

Creativity: context and interactions related to, 6; cultural perspective of, 7–8; definition of, 6; mindfulness of, 8; need for workforce adaptability and, 2–6; opportunities and choice components of, 18–21; reflection as key to understanding, 7; role of environment in, 6–8; role that society plays in, 9; teams and collaboration role in, 7. *See also* Innovation; Teaching creativity

Credit hours: changing emphasis on, 98–99; FSU BIS program flexibility toward, 163; traditional importance of, 98

Cross, P., 98, 139

Csikszentmihalyi, M., 6, 7, 9, 10, 35

Cubberley, E., 26

Cullen, R., 22, 84, 105, 193, 197

Cultural context: Bosnian female students' experience with, 54; of postmodern education, 54–56; structures or frames of references in, 55–56

Culture: creating an assessment, 100–101; creativity from interaction of society, individual, and, 10;

creativity in context of, 7–8; diversity within Israel, 7–8; respecting current institutional, 78

Culture of assessment, 100–101

Curricular change: AACP recommendations for, 40–41; accrediting bodies and, 39–42; challenge of promoting, 38–39; challenges inherent in making, 73; strategies for reducing threat of, 76–83; time has come for, 45–46, 159–160; why the need for, 1–2, 209–210. *See also* Curricular implementation; Curriculum reform; Education reform

Curricular implementation: adopting a Rogerian approach to, 73–76; adopting learner-centered attitudes and behaviors, 85–90; downplaying credit hours for, 98–99; engaging in conversations about the possibilities of, 90–93; focusing on structure for, 97–98; infusing assessment into, 99–103; using nonthreatening vocabulary for, 93–94; preparing faculty for, 83–85; reducing threat of change by compatibility approach to, 76–79; reducing threat through profitability, 79–83; rethinking prerequisites for, 94–95; rewriting course descriptions for, 96–97; timing issues of, 99; transition to learner-centered culture for, 92–93. *See also* Curricular change

Curriculum: Bruner's description of ideal, 35; definition of, 24; historic development of vocabulary referring to, 93–94; history of development, 24–28; substituting "academic plan" for, 94; transformative, 63

The Curriculum (Bobbitt), 24

Curriculum design: Bruffee on designing around set of occurrences, 97; content knowledge as center of, 28; content versus process argument

Student Rating of Instruction (SRI) [IDEA Center], 177
Students: choice provided to, 18–21, 68; contemporary approach to determining potential of, 30; declining test scores on creativity by, 5; four areas of preparation for, 2–3; "illusion of comprehension" by, 9, 103; sharing power with, 18–21, 65, 66–68
Sukhbaatar, J., 39
Sum, P. E., 150–151
Summative assessments: artistic and creative work projects, 149–150; portfolios, 148–149; presentations, 146–147; research projects, 149–150; written works, 144–146
Sun Microsystems, 4
Survey instruments, 153–154
SurveyMonkey, 177
Svinicki, M. D., 9, 20, 36, 48, 49, 52, 67, 75, 103
Syllabus Assessment Matrix, 105, 106t, 122
Sylwester, R., 35

T

Tagg, J., 23, 31, 34, 37, 50, 82, 98
Taiwan's National Chengchi University, 11
Taxonomy of knowledge, 93
Taylor, F. W., 24, 26
Teacher as gardener metaphor, 46–47
Teacher wall concept, 203–204
Teaching creativity: behaviors that foster creative environment, 11–12; examining feasibility of, 6–12; intentionality role in, 8. See also Creativity; Education technology; Faculty
Technology: changes brought about through, 159; educational tools available through, 160–161. See also Education technology; Internet
Tegrity, 164, 165
Terenzini, P. T., 39

Territoriality (academic discipline), 28–29, 190–191
Thompson, J., 192
Tierney, W. G., 27, 77
TracDat, 178
Transformative curriculum, 63
Tufts University, 166
Turf wars, 32–33, 190
Twigg, C., 176
"Twin sins of design," 62
Twitter, 165–166
Tyler, R., 26
Tyler Rationale, 26–27

U

University of California, San Diego, 202
University of Georgia, 11
University of Iowa, 198
University of Massachusetts Physics Education Research Group, 174–177
University of Minnesota–Twin Cities, 185
University of Oklahoma, 11
University of Pennsylvania, 188
University of Wisconsin-Madison, 172
Used-care metaphor, 153
Usher, R., 54

V

VandenPlas, J. R., 176
Volkwein, J. F., 39
von Glaserfeld, E., 35

W

Waldmann, S., 61
Wasserman, J., 129
Web 2.0 technologies, 161
Weigel, V. B., 167
Weigle Information Commons (University of Pennsylvania), 188
Weimer, M., 84, 96
Weinstein, C. S., 193
West, J. A., 160, 169–170

West, M. L., 160, 169–170
Western University (WesternU):
examining learner-centered design
at, 107; recursion practiced at, 108;
renovation of campus, 201; "visible
sense of community" at, 117–118
WesternU PharmD program: assessment practice at, 120–121; community building as feature in,
117; recursion practiced at, 108;
richness of curriculum at, 114;
technology-enhanced lecture hall
of, 196
Wharton, C., 187
What if? conversations, 90–93,
135
White, E. K., 189–190
White, J., 57
"Why redesign curricula?," 1–2,
209–210
Wigfield, A. L., 20
Wiggins, G., 26, 50, 51, 52, 53, 62, 68,
69, 70–71, 107, 123, 131, 133, 135,
136, 141, 149
Wikis, 166
Wilen-Daugenti, T., 161, 162

Willingham, D., 35, 48, 143
Willis, H., 166
The Wingspread Group on Higher
Education, 22, 30
Woolfolk, A. E., 193
Word journals, 141–142
Workforce: call for creativity and
adaptability in, 2–6; four areas of
preparation for, 2–3
Workforce performance, IBM Global
Services survey on, 4–5
Write to Learn movement, 137–138
"Writing as a Mode of Learning"
(Emig), 137
Written works assessment, 144–146

Y
Yearwood, E., 76
Yee, R., 188
Young, R. E., 74, 75, 103

Z
Zimbardo, P. G., 193
Zimmerman, B. J., 13
Zull, J., 35
Zygmont, D., 92